BENEATH THE LAKELAND FELLS

BENEATH THE LAKELAND FELLS

Cumbria's Mining Heritage

by the Cumbria Amenity Trust Mining History Society

RED EARTH PUBLICATIONS

1992

Copyright © Text 1992 named authors
Copyright © Photographs 1992 named contributors
Copyright © Maps 1992 A & S Thomas
Copyright © Line drawings 1992 P Fleming

ISBN 0 9512946 3 6

Published by RED EARTH PUBLICATIONS
7 Silver Street, Marton, Ulverston, Cumbria
LA12 0NQ

Printed in Great Britain by
SMITH SETTLE
Ilkley Road, Otley, West Yorkshire, LS21 3JP

ACKNOWLEDGEMENT

The authors and publishers would like to thank the many people who, through their dedication and goodwill, have made this book possible. The book is the culmination of several years' work, patient research, and photographic techniques tried, tested, and undertaken sometimes in atrocious conditions.

We would like to thank the members of the Cumbria Amenity Trust Mining History Society and the Cumbria Ore Mines Rescue Unit whose names do not appear in the book but who have contributed behind the scenes - transporting equipment and giving their assistance to the photographers, contributing their own research, and helping on the administrative side. We would also like to thank Anton and Sheila Thomas for their work on the maps.

We would like to offer our thanks to Mr Bert Whalley, of Ulverston, for developing and printing many of the plates, Cumbria Record Office (Barrow) and Dalton Castle Archive for permission to use the Furness mining collection, J & E Forder for allowing us to reproduce two of their prints, and the Barrow Mountaineering & Ski Club for the use of the Coppermines hut as a base camp and meeting place.

To conclude, the publishers would like to extend their thanks to the curators of the Caldbeck Mining Museum and members of the Mines of Lakeland Exploration Society for their assistance with the photographs in the Barytes chapter.

Cover photographs - Taylor's Level, Coniston Copper Mines *(Mike Mitchell)*, Back Strings, Levers Water, Coniston Copper Mines *(Ian Matheson)*.

Frontispiece - Old Engine Shaft wheel pit, Red Dell, Coniston *(Peter Fleming)*.

CONTENTS

Introduction	9
COPPER	11
WAD	43
SLATE	55
IRON	85
WOLFRAM	107
LEAD & ZINC	117
COAL	149
BARYTES	165
Glossary of Mining Terms	182
Bibliography	185
Index	188

INTRODUCTION
by Mike Mitchell

This book has been compiled by members of the Cumbria Amenity Trust Mining History Society in recognition of the contribution made to the industrial revolution by the metal miners of Cumbria and the Lake District, not forgetting the men who worked in coal and slate. It can, of course, also apply to other parts of the country, but in many ways the Lake District is unique. Many thousands of people visit this area each year to climb the mountains, sail the lakes, and enjoy the views - and the vast array of picture and guide books in the shops extol the splendour of the scenery and villages.

The main influence in the Lakeland area is that of the Lake District Special Planning Board and the National Trust, who are at pains to point out to visitors that the National Park is not like a municipal park but a living, working environment, with private and public landowners whose rights must be respected. But these same bodies in many ways strive to urbanise the Park by erecting new fences, notices, and even parking meters, more and more each year - bulldozing and landscaping mining sites to remove all traces, forgetting - or worse - ignoring the parts those sites have played in the economy and culture of the area.

But what do the visitors, and the residents in some cases, know of the origin of the villages? And what, they ask, are those awful scars and holes on the otherwise "unspoilt" fellside? They are mostly unaware that the villages and towns of Glenridding, Coniston, Keswick, Elterwater, Millom, Nenthead, Alston, and many more, owe their origin to mining of one form or another. Those scars, with occasional derelict buildings, are monuments (as surely as Nelson's Column and the Cenotaph) to the men, women, and children who toiled and sometimes gave their lives to win the minerals from the earth - minerals of iron, lead, copper, zinc, and coal that enabled Telford to build his iron bridge, Brunel to build his Great Eastern, and Nelson to have cutlass and cannon - not catapult!

Virtually everything we accept as normal goods in our everyday lives, from space travel to surgery, owes its origins to these miners and their descendants. Fortunes were made and lost (mostly lost) in metal mining, and there were many personal tragedies in the industry which would make national news by today's standards. But the choice was easy in those days - if you didn't work you starved!

It is time to recognise and honour the people whose lives were less than ideal in these idyllic surroundings and stop the further destruction of the few remaining artefacts.

COPPER

by Peter Fleming

In the context of world history, the "copper age" began in Mesopotamia as long ago as the 7th Century BC, when copper in its native form was discovered to be malleable and durable. It could be shaped when beaten with stone hammers. The earliest copper artefacts ever found were beads, pins and awls. It was two-thousand years before this craft reached south eastern Europe. By this time simple food vessels formed from beaten copper sheets were in use and axe heads and spear heads were being produced.

The word copper comes from the latin *cyprium* meaning "ore of Cyprus". It is believed that copper smelting was developed as early as 6000 BC in Iran. In Crete, small pieces of azurite have been discovered in a habitation layer dated to the same period. The ladies of ancient Egypt used powdered malachite in their make-up.

The first actual record of copper mining, again in Mesopotamia, is dated to 3500 BC. Across the other side of the world, copper artefacts have been discovered in Peruvian tombs of 2000 BC. These facts support the long held theory that the middle eastern and South American cultures were centuries ahead of the European Stone Age. Recent discoveries in certain copper mines in North Wales look like proving this belief to be incorrect. In 1988, stone tools, bones and traces of firesetting were found in underground workings on Great Ormes Head, and at Parys Mountain and Cwmystwyth Mine. From charcoal taken from these sites, the British Museum has carried out carbon 14 dating tests which suggest the workings on Great Ormes Head could date from between 1000 BC and 1800 BC, whilst those on Parys Mountain, Anglesey, are from 2000 BC. It seems that this part of our history may have to be revised.

So copper in its native form was the first metal used by man. Later, oxidised zones of copper deposits must have attracted attention where they came to surface - the "outcrop" as it is known - with blue and green carbonates (azurite and malachite) being quite obvious. These two minerals have been used from even earlier times to make jewellery and for painting. To obtain metallic copper from these ores was a simple matter of supplying heat with wood or charcoal using a primitive bellows. After the miners had exploited the outcrops they were naturally led to work the cupriferous lodes in depth where, instead of decomposed ore, altered by the weathering action of air and percolating rain water, they met with an unaltered substance of shining brassy-yellow colour called copper pyrites (chalcopyrite), also known as yellow sulphide of copper because it consists of a combination of copper and sulphur with an equal portion of iron.

The techniques of copper smelting had reached Britain by the beginning of the 2nd century BC. To produce metal from copper pyrites was not straightforward. How did man learn to smelt these copper sulphides and how did the ancient copper smiths become aware that these ores must be roasted in contact with air before smelting, in order to remove the sulphur content? A reasonable theory is that potters using copper minerals to produce coloured glazes hit upon the technique by accident. Doubtless the process was established after a long period of experiment.

There is no evidence, either scientific or documentary, to prove that mining took place in the Lake District prior to the early part of the 13th century when Goldscope Mine, at Newlands near Keswick, was worked for copper, as recorded in the close rolls of Henry III. It would be reasonable to think, however, that the Romans could have been active in the Caldbeck Fells and very likely in the Coniston Fells as well.

Consider again for a moment the recent discoveries mentioned previously in North Wales and bear in mind that two major Neolithic stone axe working sites are located in central Lakeland, on the Langdale Pikes and on the Scafell Range. It may yet be proved that the early "entrepreneurs", using their stone tools, worked the copper veins that would, at that time, have outcropped so obviously on the surface.

As recently as October 1991, stone mortars were found on a site at Coniston Copper Mines. This area will be more thoroughly investigated in the near future.

The copper mines of the Lake District are to be found almost entirely in the Skiddaw slates. Notable exceptions are the Coniston Copper Mines, which lie within a volcanic area of hard rhyolite. The mineral deposits found within both these areas occur in the faults and fissures caused, it is believed, by upward pressures of an underlying granite mass. These cracks were filled by circulating, mineral bearing, solutions (which may have been either hot or cold) during the Carboniferous period. Owing to the almost vertical inclination of these faults, the mines that developed on the richer ore bearing veins went very deep - 700 feet at Goldscope and over 1600 feet at Coniston. These sort of depths presented considerable problems to the miners of one-hundred years ago.

By far the most common copper ore mined in the Lake District is the brass-yellow chalcopyrite (a sulphide). Bornite, or peacock ore, which displays beautiful variegated colours, is also a sulphide and has been found at the Dalehead, Goldscope, and Coniston mines in recent years.

The two carbonates, malachite and azurite (green and blue respectively), occur in the oxidised zones near to the surface and were both exploited. Each contains around 55% copper. Hydrous silicate of copper (chrysocolla), an attractive turquoise mineral, has been found mainly in the Caldbeck mining field and to a lesser extent at Coniston.

It is generally accepted that the mining of copper in Lakeland did not start in any significant way until the arrival of mining experts from Germany in 1563. Queen Elizabeth I granted an indenture on the 10th December 1564 to Thomas Thurland, their English mining agent, and his German protege, Daniel Höchstetter, which permitted them to dig for ores throughout the land. The richest copper mine known at that time in Lakeland was named by the Germans "Gottesgab" (God's Gift), which became corrupted into "Goldscope", the name it is known by today. They started at Easter 1565, and working on a vein up to 9 feet thick. By 1568 the Company of Mines Royal had been formed. The mines of the Caldbeck Fells received a first mention in the company accounts for this year.

The Company had an ingenious way of paying their miners. Everything they used, from candles to clothing and food, was deducted from their earnings automatically, so that they avoided the difficulties of trading locally with money they did not understand. They tended to be rather independent and isolated. Most of them lived on Vicar's Island in Derwentwater, later known as Derwent Island, which they purchased for £60 in 1569, but gradually they began to integrate with the local people. Many marriages were recorded between the girls of Keswick and the miners, and their Germanic names can still be traced today - for example, Moser, Parker and Senogles. The Company spent lavishly in the locality of Keswick, chiefly on the development of the copper and lead mining areas. Smelt mills were erected to treat the ore and a whole network of packhorse trails was set up to transport the ores and the charcoal to smelt them. To produce this charcoal, Borrowdale, along with other valleys, was denuded of its trees. So good were the terms of payment to such a previously impoverished district, that prosperity was brought to many, and lucrative jobs provided for many more, whose previous existence had been limited to scraping a living from fell farming or simple rural trades.

The Keswick Journal for 1659 contains reference to the Germans working a copper mine on the west shore of Buttermere and this can still be traced today. In the Newlands Valley other copper mines worked at this time included Dalehead, Castlenook, and the nearby Longwork and St Thomas' Work. Over the ridge of Maiden Moor, to the east in Borrowdale, two copper veins had not escaped the notice of the Mines Royal. These were the Manesty Vein, otherwise known as the Saltwell Mine, and tthe Copperplate Vein, not far from Grange in Borrowdale.

The largest production area for copper other than Goldscope was undoubtedly in the Caldbeck Fells. Some of the larger mines were Roughtongill Mine, Mexico Mine, Silver Gill Mine, and Red Gill Mine, famous for its rare, deep azure blue crystals of linarite, a sulphate of copper and lead, specimens of which can be seen in the Natural History Museum. In addition to copper, considerable tonnages of lead were extracted from these mines.

It was some time after 1590 that the Company of Mines Royal discovered, or rediscovered, some of the numerous and extensive copper veins at Coniston. Traces of their work can still be seen in the lower and upper parts of Red Dell in the form of hand driven "coffin" levels. The lower working, known as Cobblers Level, was probably the first crosscut driven into the rich Bonsor Vein. The higher one was driven to work a small, isolated vein known as God's Blessing. Both these tunnels have, at a later date, been widened with explosives to accommodate wheelbarrows. The Germans would also undoubtedly have worked on the veins outcropping at Levers Water.

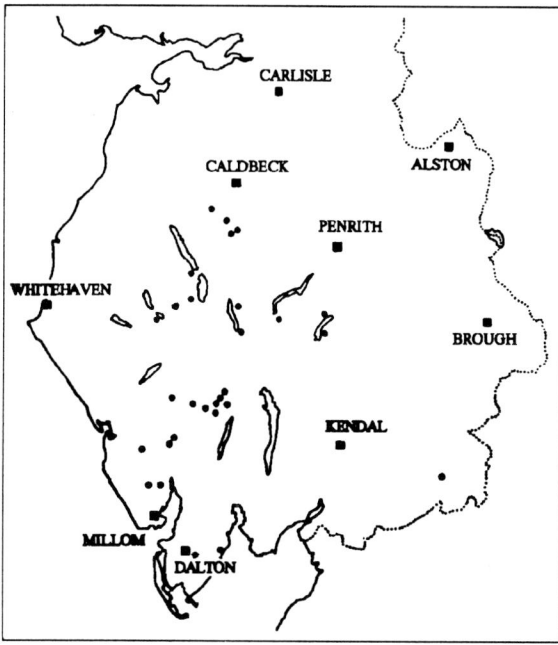

The general disposition of copper mines in Cumbria

The opening up of Coniston Mines came too late to save the Company of the Mines Royal. The parent company, Haug Laugnaure and Co, the Augsburg firm who financed the mining operations in the Lake District, were heavily in debt and had already handed over their interests to the English shareholders and those of the Germans who had chosen to remain here. This included the Höchstetter family, who, it is recorded, put forward

13

the idea of building a smelter at Coniston to avoid the long packhorse trail to the Keswick smelters with the ore. This idea was never pursued.

Mining continued until the outbreak of civil war in 1642. Little seems to have been done during the rest of the 17th century, but Greenburn Mine, situated in Little Langdale, appears as a producer of copper for the first time. It is also interesting to note that gunpowder was introduced in the Coniston Mines in 1694. Goldscope was going through a lean period with only sporadic activity. The longest period of continuous work was between 1680 and 1690. The mines in the Caldbeck Fells had declined before the outbreak of the Civil War and were reported as "left and given over".

Reasons were various. Some blamed the loss on the death of the first generations of German artisans, and their descendants not possessing the same skills. But more significant was the scarcity of timber to produce charcoal. The land had been stripped, and the visual impact must have been considerable. It took half an acre of trees to provide the charcoal for each ton of ore smelted. It was even planned to import timber from Ireland. Commonwealth troops were alleged to have destroyed the Keswick smelters and associated works. They were left "ruinated and spoyled".

This state of affairs lasted throughout the first half of the 18th century despite numerous leases having been taken out with landowners, both at Coniston and Caldbeck. However, in 1758 the Macclesfield Copper Company was formed under the directorship of Mr Charles Roe. This Company was to spend the next thirty-seven years working on the rich Bonsor Vein, at Coniston, taking it down below the old German workings, which were in excess of 150 feet below the surface. Charles Roe built a waterwheel to drive a pump and raise ore up a narrow and constricted shaft within the vein itself. It is still possible today to see the deep grooves cut into the footwall where the heavy chains constantly rubbed. This was the Bonsor East Shaft. During the first ten years of operation the output averaged one-hundred tons of finished copper per year. Work was also going on at Paddy End and Tilberthwaite mines during this period. With gunpowder now in general use, the driving of tunnels and winning of ore was speeded up considerably.

By 1795 the Macclesfield Company workings had reached a depth in excess of three-hundred feet below the surface, and the company decided, wrongly as it later proved, to abandon the mine as unproductive. The man who proved them wrong was John Taylor, the famous mining engineer, who had extensive experience in the mining fields of Devon, Cornwall, and Derbyshire. He came to Coniston in 1824 and was to transform the mines into the largest and most profitable copper mines in the north.

John Taylor signed a lease with the landowner, Lady le Fleming of Rydal Estates, giving him the rights to "use all lawful means for the finding, discovering, winning, working or getting mines of copper ore and minerals within the Lordship of Coniston belonging to Anne le Fleming". A royalty of "one twelfth part of all washed metals or minerals to be gotten out of the mine" was payable.

Taylor was soon driving new access tunnels to the Bonsor Vein in Red Dell. One of these still bears his name, another was named Fleming's Level after Lady Anne le Fleming. Level driving was also proceeding in the Paddy End Mine below the old German workings. In 1825 Taylor started his most ambitious and expensive project, the driving of a deep adit level from the lowest practical point. This area, behind the present day youth hostel, became the main ore dressing floor in the Copper Mines Valley. The adit level became known as the Deep, or Horse, Level and eventually extended beneath the Red Dell (Bonsor) and Paddy End workings. With its various branches it was to become one-and-a-half miles long, and de-water a vast area of workings. It also served as an excellent tramway for horse-drawn wagons from all parts of the mine.

Taylor also constructed a system of leats to provide

water power for winding, pumping, and dressing. Water was drawn from Levers Water, Low Water, and Red Dell and directed through three miles of leats, the same water powering waterwheels at Triddle, Paddy End, and at Bonsor Works.

On the 1st October 1834 John Taylor signed a new lease to include Richard Gaunt and John Barratt. Barratt, formerly an employee, had now become a partner and mine manager. About this time work was started on what is now known as the Old Engine Shaft, which eventually replaced the Bonsor East Shaft used by Charles Roe. As the workings got deeper on the Bonsor Vein, more efficient means of extraction and pumping were required. Work was also underway on the Triddle Shaft and in 1844 the sinking of the New Engine Shaft was begun, along with the construction of a stone incline, which is used as a pathway by fell walkers today. Meanwhile, at Paddy End, further extensive development work was being carried out. In 1840 Levers Water Mine was started and it is recorded that ninety-seven children were employed in mineral dressing in 1842, the youngest being six years old.

It is perhaps appropriate at this point to quote extracts from a contemporary account written by Dr Alexander Craig Gibson, who was the medical officer at the mines between 1844 and 1851. It was written in 1848 and provides a fascinating insight into the working methods and conditions at the time.

High up on the mountainside, you may notice a solitary waterwheel which, from having nothing near it visible from below, appears to be spinning away like a child's toy mill without aim or object. It is at the top of the main shaft, and is employed in hoisting those kibbles and water to the horse level.

And now having arrived at the works, before examining the details of the dressing process, suppose you take a subterranean ramble, and see how and where the ore is obtained, and to do that comfortably, it were well to borrow some regular habiliments to save your clothes - the gentlemen below stairs will excuse your appearing amongst them in full dress.

It will be wise to select the oldest and most extensive part of the mines for exploration, and it is that most to the east, so when you are properly equipped and have procured candles and a guide, proceed at once to the horse level mouth, light your candles, open the door and walk in.

When you have progressed thus with your crest lowered for some distance, you may straight your back and look up, for you are under the "Cobblers hole" a tremendous chasm, from which a vein of copper, extending to above the waterwheel you saw on the hillside, has been wrought, and when you are advanced about a quarter of a mile into the level, you are at the side of the shaft which reaches from the said waterwheel through all the workings down to the deepest level, and by which kibbles containing the ore are hoisted a few fathoms above your head, and there emptied into a large hopper, the mouth of which is six or seven feet above the level, and under it the wagons are run to be loaden. If you are determined to descend the shaft, it must be by a series of ladders, with wooden sides and iron steps, and you come to a platform, or "landing" at every few fathoms. Diverging occasionally from but generally following the line of the shaft, you pass several old "bunnins" - I am not sure about orthography, but the derivation is, I fancy, from "bound in" - which are short logs of wood jammed between the opposite walls of rock for the miners to stand upon when working in such situations. As you proceed on your perilous journey, you must not allow the thundering echoes of the distant blast, or the astounding rattle of the rapidly descending kibble and its chain, to deprive you of your presence of mind, else you are "but a dead tourist". But supposing that you carry your senses along with you, and are resolved to stop at nothing short of the deep workings, you continue, sometimes crawling down the ladder, and sometimes stepping cautiously across the landings, you pass several levels in your descent - viz, one twenty fathoms down, one thirty five, one fifty, and at length you arrive at the seventy fathom, when you are somewhere about the level of the village, or about four hundred and twenty feet below the place where you commenced your underground knight errantry - or, again, about six hundred and forty feet below the top of the

15

shaft. There is, "at the lowest depth a lower still", some twenty fathoms below this, another working, called "the ninety", but you are already deep enough for any useful purpose. Moving a short way onwards, you come in sight of two men working upon a "bunnin", and looking, according to your notion, very much like the inhabitants of a still lower region, the darkness being made barely visible by a couple of twinkling candles plastered against the rock with clay. Their attitudes are somewhat picturesque, as they hold up and turn the jumper with the left hand, whilst they keep driving it into the flinty rock by an incessant rapping with a hammer held in the right. Having bored their holes to a sufficient depth, they proceed to clear them out with an iron instrument something like a yard long needle, with its point bent and flattened - first scraping out the borings or fragments of stone, with the point, and then drying the hole with a small wisp of straw, or dried grass, drawn through the eye and worked up and down in the hole until all the moisture is completely mopped up. They then fill a tin tube with gunpowder, and conveying it into the hole withdraw the tube and leave the hole filled to one third, or one half its depth with powder. Having corked down, by way of wadding, the wisp used in drying, and carefully cleaned away any stray grains of powder which may possibly adhere to the sides, they next thrust a long sharpened rod of copper, called a "pricker", down one side into the powder, and pass an iron "stemmer", or ramrod, grooved on one side to fit the pricker, to feel whether it works easily, which it will not do, if the pricker is improperly inserted. They then beat in with the stemmer, a quantity of soft rotten stone called "stemming", sufficient to fill up the hole, finishing off with a little clay, and commence with the withdrawal of the pricker, an operation of some nicety. Having got it out, they pass down the hole it leaves a long straw filled with powder, having a piece of match paper attached to its outer extremity and having secured their tools, and uttered two or three indescribable warning shouts, the precise sounds of which it is difficult to realise, but which consist of the monosyllable "fire", they ignite the touch papers and immediately retire to a respectable distance, and you have better retire with them, to await the report, which, when it does occur, will be pretty likely to make you jump an inch or two out of your skin. Returning to their working, they note carefully the effects of the blast, and breaking up the larger fragments, and beating down any loose pieces that may hang about the sides, they select a suitable "lofe" and recommence boring. About three blasts in this hard rock is considered a fair day's work, the men working eight hours a day in shifts - which does not mean that they array themselves in chemises to work in, but that they are relieved or shifted at the end of eight hours, by other workmen taking their places.

And now having visited the depth of the mines, and witnessed the most important, as well as the most common of the underground operations, and moreover, being almost "sconfished" with the powder smoke, you are anxious to return to the blessed light of day, and "heaven's untainted breath", and may clamber up the interminable ladders you descended by. What you have seen, of course, conveys no adequate idea of the extent of the mines, for these hills are almost honeycombed by levels and other workings, but you have seen enough to show you the nature of copper mining. It is rather extraordinary that the mines, even in their deepest parts, are infested by myriads of rats, and why they harbour there, or what they get to eat, would require a longer head than mine to discover.

It says much for the excellent arrangements on the part of the management, that, notwithstanding the dangerous nature of the work, and the number of hands employed, serious accidents are of very rare occurrence, and when they do occur, they are almost always the result of negligence, frequently involving disobedience of orders, on the part of the sufferer. However one of the most melancholy that has yet occurred, was purely accidental, and I may relate it as a sad episode in mining life. A father and son - Irishmen - named Redmond, were employed at the foot of a shaft, "filling kibbles". The father's kibble had descended, and he had unhooked the chain, handing it to his son to attach to his kibble, which was full, and commenced refilling, when his attention was attracted by a cry, and, starting round, he saw his son carried with the kibble rapidly up the dark shaft. He called to him to hold on by the bucket, but that was considered hopeless by the workmen about, because the shaft is tortuous and the sides very rugged and uneven. A very short time showed that they were correct, for the unfortunate youth's body was heard tumbling down the shaft. The old man placed himself below, stretching out his arms to catch the body as it fell, and was with difficulty dragged from the position where he would have shared the fate of his son, whose mangled body fell close to his feet.

And now, having safety returned to this everyday world, you may examine the process through which the ore has to pass, before it is fit for the market, for, unlike most other mining, one half of the work is not done when it is brought above ground. Well, first, you perceive, it is thrown from the wagons into a heap, where water runs over it, and by cleaning the lumps, shows more plainly what each piece is made of. Then from the heap it is raked by men to a platform, or long low bench, along which a number of little boys are actively engaged in picking or separating the richer pieces from the poorer, and it is highly amusing to watch the expertness and celerity with which the imps make the selection and toss each lump into its proper receptable. The richest portion is carried at once to the crushing mill, the poorer is thrown into another shed below, to be broken up and further picked, and the mere stones are wheeled off to the rubbish heap. The ore being broken small is thrown into a crushing mill, and passed once or twice through it, being returned to the mill by an endless chain of iron buckets, which dip into the heap of crushed ore below, and carry it up, empty themselves into the mill. When ground to the size of coarse sand, the ore is carried to the "jigging troughs", which are large square boxes, filled with water, and having each a smaller box, with a grated bottom, suspended in it to a beam above, and filled with ore, a "jigging" motion being imparted to the grated boxes by water power. This jigging under the water causes the grains of pure ore, which are heavy, to sink and pass through the grating of the inner box, and the particles of spar and rock, which are lighter, to rise to the top, where they are scouped off and wheeled away to undergo another pounding and washing. The pounding is effected by means of two long rows of stamps or heavy iron shod pestles, kept incessantly rising and falling in beds fronted with perforated iron plates, and fed with the material, and a flow of water to wash it, when fine enough, through the holed plate. It is, after that, collected to go through the process of "buddling", which consists of laying it on slanted shelves, at the head of long wooden troughs, also slanting longitudinally, and a limited stream of water being allowed to run through it and wash it slowly off the shelves and down the inclined troughs, the heavier and valuable portion remains at the head, whilst the lighter and worthless portion is washed down to the lower end. All the waste water used in any of the dressing processes is made to flow through a series of large tanks or reservoirs, in which it deposits all the fine particles of ore that may be floating away, and from these tanks some thousands of pounds worth of ore is collected annually in the form of slime, and looking like bronze, which with all the other ore, is shipped to Swansea to be smelted.

Elsewhere in Lakeland copper mines were on the decline once again. Goldscope was still working but producing only lead. A small tonnage of copper was recorded from the Roughtongill mines at this time, but most of the ore extracted here was also lead. The Copperplate Mine in Borrowdale was reopened but little was done. Birkside Gill Mine, above the waterfall north of Dunmail Raise, was in production, as were two small copper mines near the northern end of Hawes Water.

Much prospecting was going on in the Duddon Valley at the following mines: Seathwaite Tarn, Cockley Beck, Logan Beck, Hesk Fell, and Ulpha Copper Mine.

At Coniston the mine was reaching its peak period. In 1849 the workings were down to 90 fathoms (540 feet) below Deep Level. The following year John Barratt began driving another Deep Level, this one in Tilberthwaite, which was to de-water the extensive old workings in the high valley to the east of Wetherlam. This level, also named Barratt's Level, was 3,000 feet long and took ten years to complete.

1856 was the year of the highest production figures for Coniston Mines. Output was 3659 tons of ore valued at £27,861. An anonymous essay, handwritten in 1858 and entitled *Coniston Mine*, gives us yet another detailed glimpse of the mine some ten years after Dr Gibson's account. The following is an extract and the original spelling has been adhered to.

Next came the Barratts which worked the mines on a large scale They drove the Deep adit level till they cut the load and then sunk the old shaft which is 1,020 ft from the Adit 300 ft more from the grass roots The work was lifted by water power the big water wheel which was 44 ft 7 in high 9 ft across the breast weight 21 tons 11cwt and 65 Horse power. the water was pumped up in 4 lifts the Bottom lift was a draw lift And the other 3 were plungers 300 ft apart. Every 40 yards down there was a drift set of which went from one shaft and the other that was 4 Stoops high that ment 10 Stoops at the rate of 4 men to Every working.

The work was drawn out at the rate of 8 trips a shift with 3 big Iron wagons which held 2 tons Each then it was dumpted down a Screen which sized it into 3 sections then it was sorted into 4 lots the first was the solid ore which was put out by itself the next was what was called Douse it was the second best the third was class quartze and copper mixed which had to go through the crushing mill to be ground to a find sand then it taken to the water sives there were 6 sets of them with 2 sives to Every Set. Each set of tubs was Emptied twice a week and Each set of tubs held 5 tons that ment 60 tons a week of jigged ore then it was put into a pile and the solid pile was ground and thrown over it so that they got a average sample. After that it was All turned over a weighed and then carted to Coniston Hall and taken to Nibthwaite by boat and then carted to Ulverston and put on rail and sent to Sent Elens.

It is interesting to learn of the rapidly deepening Old Engine Shaft, now down to 1,020 feet below Deep Level, which is 100 feet below sea level. At approximately every 20 fathoms, (160 feet), levels were driven off to extract the ore from the Bonsor Vein.

The figures quoted for those employed in the mines seem rather high. Over the previous twenty years many cottages had been built in rows overlooking Coniston village to house the mining families, but they would hardly accommodate an extra thousand people as suggested in the essay.

The mines were so productive that it was decided in 1858 to construct a branchline from the Furness Railway at Foxfield, thus doing away with the slow, laborious carting and boating of the ore via Coniston Lake to Ulverston Canal. This means of transport had been in use since the destruction of the Keswick smelters in the mid-17th century. This railway line opened on 18th June 1859.

The output of copper ore during the 1860s began an irreversible decline. In 1860 it was less than 3000 tons of dressed copper per annum and four years later had dipped below 2000 tons. The workings on the great Bonsor Vein were so deep that the cost of maintaining services, hoisting, timberwork and pumping, etc. was mounting. Up to sixteen waterwheels were said to be operating around 1870. To add to the problems, the magnetite content of the ore was increasing below the 170 fathom level, and this was very difficult to separate during dressing operations at that time.

Elsewhere in the Lake District, copper mining had almost ceased. Carrock End Mine had produced copper in 1863 and Red Gill Mine had raised only forty-five tons of dressed copper ore between 1861 and 1871. The famous Roughtongill Mine struggled on suffering heavy losses, because of extensive but fruitless development work, and finally closed in 1878.

The miners of old had missed very little in their search for minerals in the Lakeland hills and dales, but there are two locations known to the author which seem to have gone unnoticed. A fairly strong vein of copper carbonate (malachite) outcrops on the south wall of Easy Gully on Dow Crags, two kilometres south-west of Paddy End Mines. The second location, noticed for the first time in October 1990, lies in the rough ground of Low Scawdell, in Borrowdale, and consists of copper oxide, tenorite and small quantities of cuprite.

The fate of copper mining in Lakeland was sealed in the 1880s when cheap imported ore was brought from foreign lands. This coincided with the introduction of compressed-air drills at Coniston in 1883, where the workings had now reached a depth of 205 fathoms (1,230 feet) below Deep Level Adit. Dynamite had also been in use since 1877, but these valuable advances in technology were of no avail. The Old Engine Shaft wheel was stopped for the last time in 1897 after the robbing of ore pillars below Deep Level had been carried out, leaving the mine in a dangerous state. In the same year the New Engine Shaft wheel and associated machinery was dismantled. Extraction of any ore left in the higher and older workings, both at Paddy End and Red Dell, carried on until the turn of the century. Again it was a case of removing supporting pillars and floors where the veins had been left for reasons of safety.

In 1908 a French company set up an electrolytic plant to process the extensive spoil heaps. This lasted until the outbreak of the First World War in 1914. The remaining waterwheels were removed for scrap in the 1930s, the last in 1939 from the Bonsor Upper Mill. Apart from some prospecting work carried out in the early 1950s, nothing more has been done. The mines were left to decay - a permanent reminder of the prosperous past, all the employment they provided, and the influence they had on the development of various Lakeland communities and Coniston village in particular.

The visitor to Lakeland today may still see much evidence of past copper mining activity in the area, mainly in the form of spoil heaps, tunnels, shafts, and ruined mine buildings. Coniston Mines are now scheduled by English Heritage as an historical monument.

There is plenty to see relating to the 19th century period of operation, including the mine office, now the Youth Hostel, and the mine foreman's house and stables, now a mountaineering club headquarters. Behind these are the settling ponds and many ruined buildings which included a saw mill, the mine laboratory, a carpenter's shop and waterwheel pits, etc. Other waterwheel pits at Bonsor East and the Old and New Engine shafts are worth visiting. The stone arched entrance portals to Gaunt's Level and Deep Level adit are still intact.

Since 1980 the Cumbria Amenity Trust Mining History Society has been very active exploring, surveying, and conserving the underground workings. Many interesting discoveries have been made deep within long-forgotten tunnels and workings. Numerous artefacts have been found, exactly as the miners left them. These include ore wagons, railways and points, windlasses, a shaft kibble, winding wheels and - amongst the smaller items - shovels, hammers, drills, prickers, tin water bottles, ore sacks, clogs, clay pipes, and candles.

In the Top Level workings at Paddy End there are still hundreds of feet of skilfully made wooden ventilation trunkings. Some of the pumping rods remain in position in the Old Engine Shaft. The most intriguing discovery was perhaps that of a joiner-made oak barrier, or dam, sealing a tunnel beneath Levers Water, which can only be reached with great difficulty. A legend had been passed down over several generations, in Coniston village, which spoke of two oak plugs used to seal Levers Water from the mine when the tarn was dammed and the water level raised. The story was not really believed, but on the 25th January 1987 it was proved to be correct when one dam was discovered. There is a record that a Coniston blacksmith was paid for the "making of dams at Levers Water and Low Water and timbering of floodgates and sodwork etc." in 1713, but it is hardly likely that this oak barrier is that old. Its precise age may never be discovered, but it continues to hold back the waters of the reservoir.

Without doubt the most spectacular sights in these mines would never have been seen by the miners of old. For well over a hundred years formations have been growing on the walls and floors of the workings in the form of blue and green copper carbonate "flowstone" deposits. The finest of these very colourful, bright "static cascades" are to be found in the remote inner reaches of Taylor's Level and in Levers Water Mine.

The beginnings of Goldscope Mine are lost in the mists of antiquity. The mine was worked during the 13th century but it was the Germans of the 16th century, under the leadership of Daniel Höchstetter, who were responsible for its development. The photograph shows Lakeland's finest example of a "coffin level", hand-driven through the tough Skiddaw slate with hammers, chisels, wedges, and perhaps the use of fire to splinter the rock. The tunnel was used for channelling water to an underground waterwheel. *(photo, Peter Fleming)*

Probably one of the most remarkable achievements of 16th century mining was the chiselling out of the waterwheel pit in Goldscope Mine. The wheel raised ore from an underground shaft and provided the power for de-watering the workings - probably by the simple means of lifting buckets from the depths. The wheel was installed, it is thought, in 1593, but was abandoned the following year when rich veins of chalcopyrite were discovered in the Coniston fells
(photo, Chris Jones)

An Elizabethan working above the Longwork, at the head of the Newlands valley. The old workings were narrow and restrictive, mainly because the rock was removed by plug and feather. Every ounce of ore won was paid for in sweat, blood, and hardship.
(photo, Dave Bridge)

Early workings at the Back Strings, above Levers Water, Coniston. Traditionally, these open workings are said to date to the Elizabethan peiod but recent discoveries in the ruined hut complex suggest they are earlier, possibly Bronze Age. *(photo, Peter Fleming)*

What appears at first sight to be just a lump of Borrowdale volcanic is in fact an early stone mortar for hand-crushing copper ore. These mortar stones, sometimes called ore-dressing stones or anvils, were in use over a very long period of time. Similar stones were used in the Bronze Age workings on Great Ormes Head, Anglesey, and on the 19th century lead dressing floors at Eagle Crag Mine, Patterdale. Dating implements such as these is virtually impossible, though expert opinion maintains that this particular example pre-dates the Elizabethan period. For scale - the clay pipe (discovered in a near-by slate quarry) is 102mm long.   *(photo, Peter Fleming)*

Coppermines Valley, as the name implies, was the centre of Coniston's mining industry. In the foreground are the cottages of Irish Row, built for immigrant miners escaping the Irish famines and land clearances of the 19th century. In the centre of the picture are the Bonsor dressing floors, the focal point of activity. The white building in the centre was once the mine office - now it belongs to the Youth Hostel Association. The cottage to the right was the manager's house and stable - now it is a mountaineering hut. To the right, Red Dell, scene of exploitation on the Bonsor Vein, ascends to the crags, while to the left the mine track winds around Kernal Crag to Grey Crag, Paddy End Mine, and the Elizabethan workings above Levers Water. *(photo, Peter Fleming)*

Holywath, Coniston, formerly the residence of John Barratt, the principal share holder in the Coniston Copper Mines. Barratt purchased the house in 1842 for £265, when it was no more than a cottage. He enlarged the building over a period of time. It is still the home of one of John Barratt's descendants, Major J W Barratt Hext. *(photo, Peter Fleming)*

The Bonsor Deep Level, or Horse Level, was driven in 1825 under the direction of the famous mining engineer, John Taylor, to intercept the Bonsor Vein, a quarter of a mile inside the southern flank of Wetherlam. Water from the deep Bonsor workings was pumped by waterwheel and reciprocating rods to discharge into the new level and flow out into Red Dell Beck. With the sinking of the Old Engine Shaft, and later the New Engine Shaft, Deep Level became the major water course of the Red Dell workings. In later years the underground ramifications of Red Dell and Paddy End were connected by an extension of the Deep Level, driven through the soft rock of the Great Crosscourse. In its entirety, Deep Level was somewhere in the region of one-and-a-half miles in length, its branches penetrating most of the major veins of the area.
(photo, Peter Fleming)

The Old Engine Shaft Waterwheel, circa 1900. The waterwheel was installed in 1834 and last operated in 1897.

Standing like a watch tower in the throat of Red Dell, the launder support for the Old Engine Shaft waterwheel is all that remains to mark the site of Coniston's largest wheel. The shaft was sunk by John Taylor around 1834 to exploit the chalcopyrite of the Bonsor Vein. For many years the great stopes of the Bonsor had been pumped dry by the wheel of the Bonsor East Shaft, situated a few yards to the left of the picture. But the Bonsor East Shaft was sunk on the vein and its route, as the mine deepened, became torturous and the pump-rods inefficient. The Old Engine Shaft was sunk to the north of the vein and descended vertically through the hard Borrowdale volcanics to intercept the mineralised ground at a depth of several hundred feet. The shaft top was situated at the end of a short tunnel a few yards to the north of the wheel pit. The reciprocating rods ran on rollers to an angle-bob, from which descended the heavy pitch-pine pump-rods, delivering motion to the pumps over a thousand feet below. The pump-rods are still in position in the upper reaches of the shaft - and the sheave winding wheel (the waterwheel also provided the notion for raising the ore) still sits in a cradle of timber above the shaft top.

In the centre of the picture are the buildings, spoil heaps, and dressing floors of the Bonsor Mine. The dressing floors were also used for processing slate from the Blue Quarry on the side of Wetherlam. *(photo, Peter Fleming)*

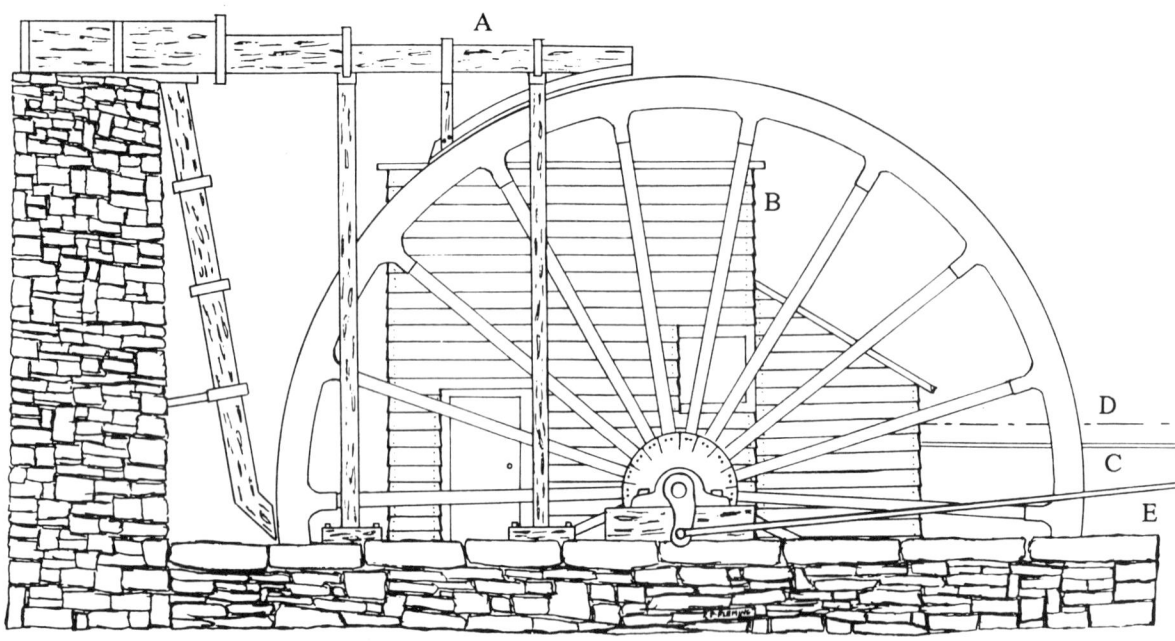

The Old Engine Shaft waterwheel - 45 feet in diameter, 100 hp, installed in 1850, last used in 1897.

- A - Wooden launder from water race.
- B - Winding machinery house.
- C - Winding rope or chain.
- D - Signal wire to shaft.
- E - Driving rod via rocking post to flat rods.
- F - Flat rods to balance bob.
- G - Sheaved winding wheel.
- H - Wooden shaft partition.
- J - Pumping rods.
- K - Weight box.

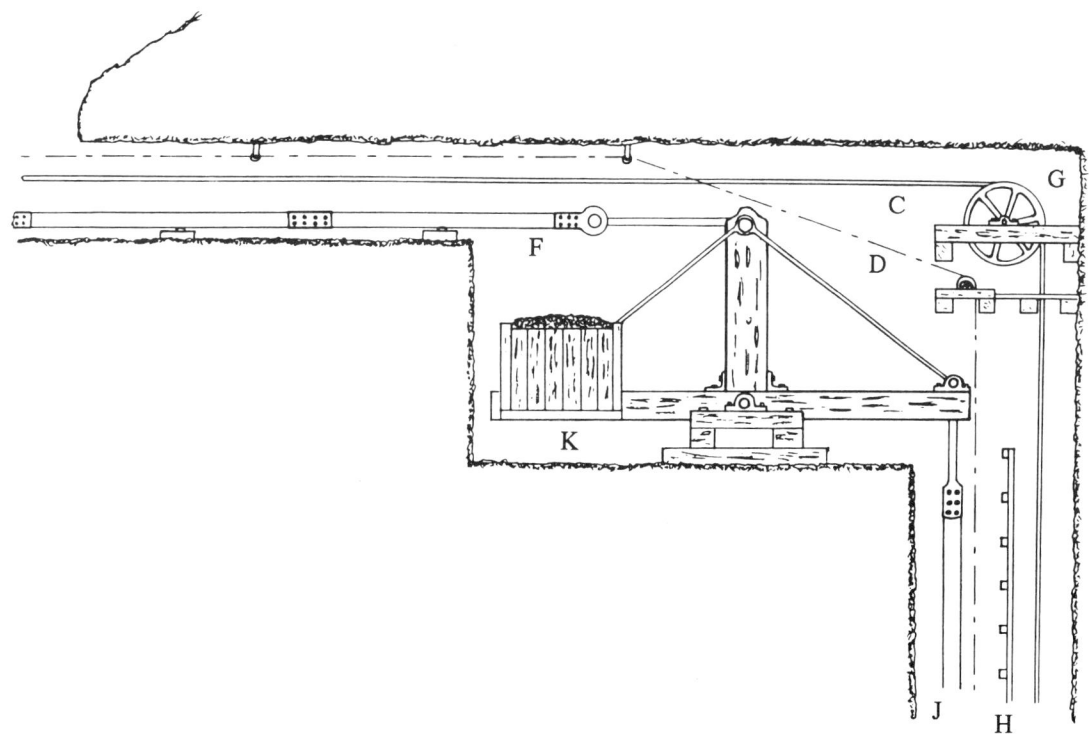

Arrangement of the balance bob at the top of the Old Engine Shaft. This shaft, 1,320 feet deep, was used for haulage and pumping, and contained a laddered manway below Deep Level. *(drawings, Peter Fleming)*

The Old Engine Shaft sheave wheel perched on its platform 300 feet above the Bonsor Deep Level, and over 1200 feet above the foot of the shaft. Here, restoration work is in progress to secure the wheel and its rotting timbers, and prevent the entire set-up plunging to destruction. *(photo, Mike F Mitchell)*

A kibble, used for hauling ore and waste from the depths of the workings. This particular example, made from two plates of iron rivetted together, was rescued from Taylor's Level. For an idea of the scale, the clay pipe is 102mm long. This kibble is small compared with the kibbles used in the larger shafts, some of which were capable of holding over a ton of ore.
(photo, Peter Fleming)

Hanging in time and space. The Old Engine Shaft pump rods remain suspended, motionless since the 1890s. This photo was taken from a tunnel at the Bonsor East Shaft top, used in days gone by as an access route to the pit-work in the Old Engine Shaft.
(Peter Fleming)

Pit props and shattered rock in the Bonsor Deep Level, a few yards to the west of the Bonsor East Shaft. This section of Deep Level dates to the late 1820s and at one time led directly into "Cobblers Hole", the richest portion of the Bonsor Vein. The timbers in the photograph are comparatively new, being installed in the 1950s when Willie Shaw, local miner and author of *Mining in the Lake Counties*, attempted to clear a way along Deep Level with a view to carrying out some prospecting in the old workings. The adventure ended in failure. *(photo, J & E Forder)*

The workings of Top Level, at Paddy End Mine, are as complex as they are extensive. This is a view up one of the near-vertical stopes on one of the veins between Stephen's Vein and the Paddy End Old Vein. Safety equipment during the 1880s - when this portion of the mine was last active - was rather rudimentary, as can be seen by the scaling chain, the means by which the miners were obliged to ascend to their working platforms high above the floor of the stope. Modern flash units illuminate the workings and give an insight into the scale of these places. The miners, who had to climb with their tools in their hands, heavy hammers under their arms, and dynamite slung in pouches, had to make do with candles. *(photo, Peter Fleming)*

High in the stopes of Paddy End Mine, seventy feet above the sole of Middle Level. Timbers, or stemples as they were called, were positioned at regular intervals to add support and prevent the stope walls from crashing in. They also provided convenient perches from which the miners could operate.
(photo, Peter Fleming)

Top Level extends for many thousands of feet into the heart of Brim Fell, the northerly flank of Coniston Old Man. Ore mined in Top Level was, during the main period of working, tipped down rises to Middle Level and trammed out to a gravity incline running down the side of Grey Crag. During the early years of working, and possibly during the final years, ore and waste were trammed along Top Level to be tipped on the fell. It is doubtful whether horses were ever used to perform this task - more likely men and boys were employed to push the heavy tubs along the twisting iron tracks.

The ore tub shown here is one of three discovered in the Coniston Copper Mines and is thought to date to the 1880s. The design is interesting because the wheels are not equidistant from the ends. The front axle has been placed close to the centre of gravity to allow ease of tipping. The rear axle is not fixed to the chassis - it floats free to render the tub manoeuvrable in tight corners.

Note in the picture on the left the "deads" stacked on the roof timbers and the gaps in the false floor beneath the wheels of the ore tub. *(photos, Peter Fleming)*

The aptly named Earthquake Passage, a branch of the Top Level workings in the Coniston Copper Mines, is a fine example of the effects of fracturing, caused by stress in the hard volcanic rock. The tunnel runs through a narrow band of rock separating the stopes of two parallel veins. The tunnel wall is slowly subsiding into the roof of the nearest stope. *(photo, Peter Fleming)*

Ventilation was a problem in most of the larger Lakeland mines. Air doors were installed to divert the flow of air through the workings but on blind drives more elaborate systems were called for. Here, in the far reaches of Coniston's Top Level, air was conveyed to the face along wooden trunking. The joiners overcame the problem of negotiating deviations by resorting to cast iron pipes, inserted into the trunking, to form angles and corners. The wooden trunking is still in place - a hundred years after it was last used. The cast iron corner sections, though, were too valuable to leave behind. *(photo, Peter Fleming)*

A jackroll, or windlass, abandoned on Top Level, Paddy End Mine, Coniston. Jackrolls have been used since ancient times for raising and lowering men and equipment, and lifting ore and even water from the depths of the mine. They were still being used as recently as the early 1900s in the Cumbrian iron mining industry, particularly in the sinking of trial shafts where they were employed in raising kibbles of waste. *(photo, Peter Fleming)*

High on the slopes of Wetherlam, on the bank at Wetherlam Mine, are the remains of the gearing system of a horse gin. Gins were capstans, wound by horses, used for raising kibbles from a shaft. The Wetherlam gin was an elaborate affair. Dating from about 1900, instead of turning a winding drum, the horse wound a cogwheel which, in turn, drove a prop shaft which raised the kibble from a winze situated inside the adit level. The gin was manufactured by John Fell & Co, of Wolverhampton, and installed by the mine operators, Thomas Warsop and Charles Edwin Day. *(photo, Peter Fleming)*

WAD

by Dave Bridge

When a descent is made from Great Gable into Borrowdale by way of Brandreth and Grey Knotts, skirting the crags of Gillercomb and turning north west down the long shoulder towards Seatoller, it is hard to imagine that beneath one's feet a famous Lake District mining industry was once in full swing. But near the place where Newhouse Gill drops steeply to join the River Derwent at Seathwaite the scene changes dramatically. Here the ground is pockmarked with shallow pits and cuttings, grassy mounds and ruined stone shelters. The debris of more extensive levels leads down to the ancient boundary wall of Seatoller Common at the 1300 ft contour where a deep pit adds to the scarring of the landscape. Beyond the wall the fellside is pierced by a series of levels or "stages". A working of great depth lies half hidden beneath a camouflage of holly, and more spoil is concealed in the small wood below.

Such intense activity in the volcanic heart of Lakeland may come as a surprise to the unsuspecting visitor. What rewards did the adventurers seek? What unheard of riches drove men to scratch and scrape at the turf and boulders to expose the bedrock beneath? If the winding miner's track is followed down the fellside a clue will be found in the form of a marker stone. This stone displays the inscription - "John Bankes Esquier 1752". The name Bankes is inseparable from the famous pencil industry of Keswick - and the mineral responsible for the founding of that industry was wad.

At least that is what the locals called it. To mineralogists wad is a dark earthy substance consisting mainly of hydrated manganese dioxide. But the Borrowdale wad is graphite, also called plumbago and earlier known as black-lead. These names disguise its true chemical nature which was determined in 1779 by the German scientist K W Scheele, though as late as 1825 Borrowdale wad was still being mistakenly called a "carburet of iron". Graphite in its pure form is carbon, less highly structured than diamond and composed of weakly bonded atomic layers. It is greasy to the touch which is due to tiny flakes or platelets rubbing off. These retain their crystalline structure and impart a metallic lustre to the deposit. Pure graphite can be machined, cut with a knife and sharpened to a point.

The working of graphite deposits is thought to have been well established by the mid 13th century in central Europe, and there is evidence that 200 years later it was used there in pottery and later in the manufacture of crucibles. In the 17th century deposits were being exploited in New England and the East Indies and possibly before that time in Spain and Mexico. Soon the occurrence of graphite in Siberia, Ceylon, and many other places, was known. Small deposits were worked in Scotland, eg. Glen Strathfarrar, and in Bannerdale where it was mined in the mid 19th century (in fact

Bannerdale pencils are said to have been made), but nowhere in the world have such large quantities of graphite of the purity of best Borrowdale wad been found.

For many years after its first discovery Borrowdale wad was used for marking sheep when it was also known as "black cawke". The development of best quality wad as a writing material from these early beginnings is of course well known, resulting in the high quality pencils of the 19th century. But its other uses have been as diverse as its many properties. It was used medicinally as early as 1693 and by 1709 was a recognised remedy for colic and for easing the pain of "gravel, the stone and strangury", when small quantities were ground up and taken in white wine or ale by country folk. As a lubricant it was exploited "for smoothing wood rollers and screws", was used on ship's rigging, and its ability to endure high temperatures, together with its resistance to thermal shock, ensured a steady demand for the lower grade material in the manufacture of crucibles and other foundry ware. A combination of these properties made it valuable as a separating layer between iron moulds and castings, in fact it was said in 1752 to answer "this Purpose better than any thing yet found out". Low grade wad was also used for polishing and protecting ironware. An important overseas market developed mainly for pencil quality wad (eg. crayons d'Angleterre) and, according to Bishop Nicolson, in Holland for glazing earthenware pots.

In other parts of the world graphite occurs in metamorphosed rocks as bedded masses (shales) or as disseminations through the country-rock (flakes) - but in Borrowdale it is associated with veins. Ward's interpretation of the geology of the area in 1876 defined eight such veins traversing an igneous dyke. He identified two types of intrusive rock, a highly altered diorite and blue trap or diabase. A more recent interpretation of Strens simplifies this to a single intrusion of diabase, the graphite being confined to a 400 metre stretch of the vein system. The richest deposits appear to have occurred at the junction of the diabase with the Borrowdale volcanics. The graphite occurs as lumps or nodules in pipes of anything up to 3 feet by 9 feet, in cross-section, and in sops (or "bellies") away from the veins, and is located by following quartz strings which often contain thin graphite coatings. The random occurrence of the deposits and the numerous false leads made wad mining a particularly frustrating affair in later years when the surface outcrops had been worked out. This is borne out by the labyrinthine nature of the workings.

There has been much argument over the origin of the Borrowdale graphite since it is not simply the result of heating and restructuring of carbonaceous material within metamorphosed sedimentary rocks, as many other graphite deposits are. In the absence of an immediate organic source the possibility of carbon from the decomposition of carbon monoxide, derived from the reduction of carbon dioxide by iron-rich silicates or pyroxenes in the diabase, was put forward by Strens in 1965. However, Firman points out that on this basis Borrowdale-type graphite should be very common. A theory first proposed by Sedgwick in 1848 is that carbon from the underlying Skiddaw slates, which contain the remains of minute forms of life from the seas of early Ordovician times (500 million years ago), was vaporised by later volcanic intrusions and redeposited. Measurements of the isotopic ratio carbon 13/carbon 12 in samples of Borrowdale graphite, reported in 1981 by Weis, Friedman and Gleason, have given this early theory new impetus but these workers propose that carbon monoxide from the reaction of superheated water vapour with the underlying carbon deposits, rather than carbon vapour itself, is the transport medium. In view of the low concentration of carbon available in the Skiddaw slates compared with the large volume of graphite in the Borrowdale vein system, which has always been a sticking point of this theory, Parnell suggests that the diabase acted as a channel for gases mobilised by other means, implying an extended period for the build up of the graphite. Nevertheless

Mitchell and Ineson in 1975 showed by potassium-argon dating that the diabase intrusion and the graphite deposition both occurred at a similar geological time (ie. late Caledonian or about 380 million years ago) and are therefore probably genetically connected.

Much of the mine's long history is clouded by folklore but since Postlethwaite several other attempts have been made to unravel the facts. William Camden's mention of "the famous mine of wad or Black-lead", after his journey through the north of England in 1582 while researching for *Britannia*, was for many years thought to be the earliest written evidence of wad mining in Borrowdale. The exact time that the wad deposits were discovered however is obscure. It is likely that the Furness monks would have known of their existence because the manor of Borrowdale was in their possession until the dissolution of Furness Abbey by Henry VIII, in 1537, but there are no known monastic records to support this view. On the premise that the monks would have put the wad to good use had they known of it an imaginative attempt was recently made to search for evidence of graphite on the only surviving manuscript from Furness Abbey - two great folio volumes of the *Coucher Book* written by the monk John Stell in 1412. But a careful inspection of the rulings and guide lines drawn in to assist the scribe revealed nothing to suggest that good quality graphite was being extracted locally in the early 15th century, although it did appear that inferior iron-impregnated material, possibly stray pieces of wad picked up from the stream bed, had been in the monk's possession.

Nevertheless there is evidence that a wad mine was established by the time of the dissolution because according to Boon the Minister's Accounts for the dissolved monastery of Furness, dated 1540-41, include 6s 8d from the profit of a mine of stone called "calkstone" otherwise "Shepe Oodde" in Borrowdale, and the mine is again mentioned in 1542-44. Then in August 1555 a visit to the manor of Borrowdale by royal commissioners Thomas Legh and Nicholas Bardsey to enquire of ores etc., including any wad-hole "for the colouring or uring of shepe" resulted in the first recorded lease of the mineral rights for wad to one Ambrose Dormer of Oxfordshire.

It is interesting that the 1555 report refers only to the "Wad hole or Cauke pyt...lyeing in the Comon of Setower" (Seatoller). This is the upper working, later called Gorton's Pipe, which outcrops on the common above the boundary wall, though it is possible that a second outcrop, Woodman's, was also being worked at the same wad hole. The report implies that the lower working or Grand Pipe some 120 yards down the slope in enclosed ground had not yet been discovered. A long held belief that wad was first discovered below a large uprooted ash (or oak) tree in Queen Elizabeth's time (ie. 1558 or after) almost certainly refers to the later discovery.

By 1565 the Company of Mines Royal had set up their copper mining industry at Keswick and German miners were beginning to arrive in the district, bringing their expertise in both mining and smelting techniques. According to the 1555 report the wad mine was badly in need of such mining skills "the said wad beyng very dangerus to get by reason of habundance of waters" and on the face of it one might expect Daniel Höchstetter, the manager of operations at Keswick, to have taken an active interest in the Borrowdale wad. The Keswick mining company's terms of reference were however carefully spelled out in a letters patent which granted the mining only of gold, silver, copper and quicksilver, and an indenture which extended this to tin, lead, precious stones and pearl, and there is no indication in the account books of the German miners up to 1577 nor in any existing inventories or reports up to 1602 that any interaction occurred between the two mining concerns, not even the use of Borrowdale graphite for crucibles in the Keswick smelthouse.

It was not until 1607 that a link was forged and the wad holes were sublet to the brothers Emanuel and Daniel Höchstetter (jnr) who had taken over the running of the Keswick industry at their father's death in 1581. This agreement however was a private affair and had nothing to do with the Company of Mines Royal, which by this time had extended its interests to the copper mines at Coniston. Although no written record of the effect of German influence on the wad mine exists we know that German miners were subsequently employed there. For example parish records show that Thomas Kalcher left Coniston for Seathwaite some time between 1610 and 1612, the year that his fourth child William was baptised. He originally came from Newlands and would have carried with him the skills and knowledge of Steffan Kalcher, an experienced pickman who had worked at the Goldscope mine in the latter part of the 16th century and was buried in Newlands in 1594. One wonders what arrangements had been made with the company (if any) for Thomas Kalcher's transfer to the wad mine.

There are good reasons to believe that the market for wad was opening up towards the end of the 16th century even though this is not reflected in the yearly rent paid to the Crown, which stood at 13s 4d from 1555 until after 1614. A lawsuit of 1597 specifically refers to both upper and lower wad holes being worked, and although the upper one was officially confined to use by manorial tenants for "the markinge or smuttinge of their sheepe and other their necessary use" and "not to sell the same or dispose of it in any other sort", there was no such restriction on the lower wad hole. Furthermore the case reveals that seven tons of superior wad worth over £13 per ton had been stored in a barn at Seathwaite, presumably awaiting shipment elsewhere. The earliest known description of a pencil, that by Gesner of Zurich in 1565, refers to the use of "a kind of lead...others call it English antimony" and Camden in 1582 described wad as a stone "which painters use to draw their lines and make pictures of one colour in their first draughts". There is also evidence that Flemish traders were supplying the Michaelangelo School of Art in Italy with Cumberland graphite by about 1580 and by 1602 the Company of Merchant Adventurers of Newcastle-upon-Tyne had deemed it necessary to add black-lead to their levy lists.

So by the time the Germans took over it is likely that work at the lower wad hole would be well advanced. It is not known when a decision was made to drain this working but the adit level called the Old Men's Stage is very old. Although now collapsed at the entrance it can be inspected by descending the Grand Pipe which it intersects about 100 ft from the top. German influence can be seen in the coffin shaped outline of parts of this level and adjacent side workings and also in telltale grooves which are characteristic of stope (wedge) and feather work. In hard rock chiselled levels could take as much as a week to progress a distance of one foot and so the 70 yards to the Grand Pipe would have taken many months, if not years, depending on the soundness of the rock. By the year 1602 English miners at Coniston were being taught the skill of driving through hard rock by their German colleagues and it is almost certain that much of the hand work in the wad mine was wrought by pickmen of English stock. Another skill which the Germans are thought to have brought to the wad mines was that of hushing or "damage", ie. washing away the surface soil to examine the rock beneath for veins and surface outcrops. This practice was not new to the district. For instance only a few years earlier visiting Crown inspectors had recommended to the Company of Mines Royal that at the Caldbeck mines "it were meet that one or more dams were made to discover the Veins at the topp".

In 1613 ownership of the wad mine changed when James I granted lands in the manor of Borrowdale to Londoners Whitmore and Vernon. They immediately sold off each of the tenancies to its occupier under the terms of the Great Deed of Borrowdale, one copy of which is dated 28 November 1614, but the wad holes were the subject of a separate transaction and became the property of local gentlemen William Lamplugh and Charles Hudson. The Höchstetter mining rights were unaffected by these transactions, but Emanuel died in

1614 and in 1625 the lease was bought by the London lawyer Sir John Bankes, son of John Bankes a wealthy Keswick tradesman. Sir John, whose residence was Corfe Castle in Dorset, had three years earlier purchased the Lamplugh share or moiety in the mine with his father-in-law Ralph Hawtrey. And so in the year 1625 the Bankes family began to work the wad mine, an association which was to last for over two centuries. But the Höchstetter connection was not completely lost because parish records show that until her death in 1622, Sir John's sister Joyce had been married to no less a person than Joseph Höchstetter, son of Emanuel, grandson of the great Daniel Höchstetter and now manager of the declining Keswick copper industry.

Though the copper industry suffered badly from the Civil War the supply of Borrowdale wad was unaffected. The nature of the deposits, ie. lumps or nodules generally varying in weight from less than 1 oz to 6 or 7 lbs, and occasionally upwards of 50 lbs, which could easily be removed by hand from the pipes and sops, and required no treatment other than washing and sorting, meant that once a rich deposit had been discovered many tons could be extracted in a short time with little expense and the market flooded. For instance after a large find in the 1760s, seven tons of wad worth about £3000 were extracted in forty-eight hours, and a workman once affirmed that he could "get the value of £1000 in half an hour". For this reason sale agreements at the time included a condition whereby to maintain the resale value the proprietors undertook not to open the mine again within an agreed period or a penalty would be imposed by the purchaser (in later years the proprietors themselves controlled the supply and continued the practice of periodic opening). A series of such bargains between the mine owners and London or Newcastle merchants during the period 1646 to 1671 each involved about seventy tons of wad with mine closure clauses of six or seven years. This wad was sold in different grades from pieces "the bigness of a hen's egg" down to pieces "the bigness of a White pea", and later in the period "the rock or fourth sort" and an even more inferior fifth sort. Over the twenty-five years the price per ton of the best grade material increased from £18 to £100.

By 1710 the mine was owned jointly by the Shepheard and Bankes families, a partnership that was to last for half a century. In that year the Old Men's Stage was reopened after a period of thirty-two years, during which time there had been no inspection of the old workings. It is not difficult to imagine the eager anticipation of the mine officials as they entered the narrow winding level, and their colourful use of the vernacular when it was revealed that thieves had been in before them and "carried on the old work, till they had lost it in the rock". Thankfully a rich new "belly" was soon discovered back from the forehead. The temporary abandonment of the lower workings does not imply that the mine had been unproductive in the latter part of the 17th century - a view popularly held. By 1690 the French possessed a navy of over two-hundred ships and the English and Dutch were endeavouring to reaffirm their command of the sea. It is known that the demand on graphite for facing the inside of cannon ball moulds was restricting supplies for pencils at that time and to close the mine completely would not make sense. Furthermore Thomas Robinson wrote in 1709 that "the vein is opened but once in seven years" which was normal practice, and there were many rich deposits still to be found in the upper wad hole.

The same year Bishop Nicolson of Carlisle, a notable scholar and historian, who five years earlier had been granted a Fellow of the Royal Society by its president Sir Isaac Newton, made the journey to Seathwaite to visit the mine and was "courteously received" by John Shepheard. The bishop took the trouble to record his observations yet it was to be another forty years before a vivid description in the Gentleman's Magazine attracted the attention of a wider public. After that the wad mine became the focal point of a long procession of tourists including the poet Thomas Gray, the travel writer William Gilpin, Captain Budworth and many others. In 1765 the French mining engineer Gabriel Jars included the mine in his *Voyages Metallurgiques* and the chemist and mineralogist Charles Hatchett in his 1796 tour of England and Scotland when visiting "mines and manufactories". Many of these left valuable eyewitness accounts.

To maintain output development work was necessary and over the years more levels were driven into the fellside. These served several purposes - exploration (by following veins or strings), drainage, ventilation and tramway access to the various deposits. Exploratory levels, notably Common and Moor stages (which produced a little wad) were eventually driven on Seatoller Common beyond the boundary wall, and a low trial was made into the side of the gill. But the main upper deposits were worked at different times from Gorton's, Harrison's and Gill stages, to be undercut finally by Farey's Stage. The upper of these four stages was extended in 1735-36 by the Gorton brothers, who may well have been related to the Swaledale mining family of that name as James Gorton, a miner of Gunnerside, had become a leaseholder of the Tilberthwaite copper mines in 1717. Gunpowder was in use by then but it is quite possible that a much earlier attempt had already been made by hand to drain the upper wad hole.

By this time the manager or "steward" was Thomas Dixon, the first of a long line of Dixons associated with the mine whose integrity and ability were much valued; "for more than fifty years he has given the most perfect satisfaction to the proprietors" was written of one of his descendants. One of his main responsibilities would be the mine's security as the stealing of wad was a perennial problem and best quality wad was soon to fetch 12s per pound or over £1300 per ton. For that reason a security lodge was built at the entrance to the upper workings where dwelt an armed guard day and night to keep an eye on the site. When the mine was opened in the 1760s the eight workmen employed there were closely watched by six overseers who frequently searched their pockets for wad. During periods of inactivity all openings were filled with waste and the precaution was taken of throwing to the bottom any poor quality wad which had not been extracted. Such caches can still be found today. The lodge situated just below the boundary wall was an elaborate affair and contained at least three rooms with a roadway passing through the building to the portal of Harrison's Stage. A smaller building was erected over the entrance to the Old Men's Stage and it became the practice during periods of closure to further protect the entrances by temporary masonry work and walling within. However pilfering of the spoil heaps was rife and could provide a comfortable subsistence for the pickers who "digging with mattocks, and other instruments" could generally clear six or eight shillings a day and sometimes more - up to ten times the wage of a farm worker or quarryman.

From a scene of clandestine operations and illicit dealings colourful characters emerge. Less well-known perhaps than the legendary smuggler Black Sal is William Hetherington who made an ambitious and successful attempt to work the wad mine from across Newhouse Gill (then known as Wadhole Gill) where in 1749 he opened a small copper level. In the timber lining of his modest working a secret door gave access to a branch which ran direct to the wad beneath his neighbour's land. He was luckier than Black Sal (who was allegedly hunted to her death by wolfhounds) and his misdemeanour landed him the job of a steward at the wad mine. A narrow level can be found amongst the rocks and bracken across the gill but if this were Hetherington's working a heavy roof fall has obliterated any evidence of his lucrative little enterprise.

And lucrative it could be for one "gang of villains" was accustomed to stealing wad worth £1000 per year - equivalent to well over £100,000 today. Greed proved to be their downfall one January night in 1751 when they attacked the lodge at the upper mine with fire arms "but losing one of their number by the fire from the place, the rest fled", an incident which together with the Hetherington affair provoked the proprietors into action. A petition to Parliament followed by a Bill guided through by John Bankes' brother Henry, who being true to the family tradition was then a Tory MP for the borough of Corfe, resulted in the much quoted 1752 Act of George II whereby stealing and receiving wad would be treated as felony and thus punishable by public whipping and a year's imprisonment with hard labour, or by up to seven year's transportation. The mounting colonial rivalry between Britain and France at the time no doubt worked in the proprietors' favour and gave the Bill a degree of urgency as the wad was still needed for the "casting of bombshells, round-shot and cannon-balls". As a further precaution John Bankes called a halt to local sales of wad. But these deterrents and the placing of marker stones about the site had little long term effect. Even as consignments of wad left the Seathwaite guard house for Kendal under armed escort on the first stage of their journey to London, lively black market trading between miners and foreign dealers was underway at The Bunch of Grapes (now the George Hotel) in Keswick, and the routes to the coast must have been as diverse as the smugglers were devious - as illustrated by a recent find of best wad in the Grisedale Pike area. The wad pickers were equally busy, for on a winter's night the flicker of as many as forty lanterns could be seen up on Seatoller Fell. According to Shelagh Sutton a shot from William Dixon's blunderbuss would "mak em run like clipt hens". In 1930 there was still a blunderbuss lying around at Seathwaite Farm.

From 1750 to 1769 the lower workings remained closed and in about 1760, according to Gabriel Jars, a new large deposit yielding £3000 worth of wad was discovered in the upper mine. The moiety of the wad mines belonging to the Shepheard family had in February 1758 been let to "several gentlemen, chiefly residing in London", who must have viewed this find with some satisfaction. When the Old Men's Stage was eventually reopened with the intention of reworking the Grand Pipe the latter became so unmanageable due to its great depth - about 200 feet below adit or some 300 feet from the surface - that the work had to be abandoned. But in 1769 Wickersley's Sop was discovered behind a rider in one of the veins yielding 177 casks of the best wad. Nine years later the "Great Opening" sop yielded 417 casks containing 70 lbs each which would be worth at least £43,000 as wad was by now fetching up to 30s per pound.

The poor quality wad from Wickersley's Sop was initially stowed on or behind bunnings in the Grand Pipe but in 1778 it was ground down to a coarse powder and thrown into the beck - a novel way of cheating the thieves. There were two more workings of existing deposits up to 1788 but after that date the prospects began to look bleak. Apart from a five ton deposit of low grade wad nothing of any size was discovered for some years, and although the company had a large stock in reserve a great deal of dead work was carried out. In 1793 Captain Budworth noted "now they are afraid the mine is exhausted", and when Charles Hatchett visited the mine in 1796 he found seven men employed and a new exploratory level being driven from surface. At that time the Bankes moiety was owned by a Henry Bankes and one of the eight shareholders of the old Shepheard moiety was Sir Joseph Bankes, a mining entrepreneur who greatly admired Hatchett's scientific abilities.

In 1793 Parliament voted overwhelmingly for a redoubling of British naval and military effort in the build-up to the Napoleonic Wars, but by that time munitions work would have had little if any impact on the demand for graphite, because in 1758 the ironmaster Isaac Wilkinson (previously of Backbarrow) had taken out a patent for "A new method or invention for casting of Guns or Cannon...in dry sand", claiming that they would be "Made and cast in a much more neat, complete, exact and useful, as well as cheap and expeditious manner than any method hitherto known or made use of". However, the cottage industry of pencil-making was quietly exerting increasing pressure on the dwindling supply of best wad, now at the inflated price of 3 gns per pound and still rising. Already John Ladyman, who left the woollen industry to make pencils soon after the year 1800, was involved with the mine. Now under considerable pressure the proprietors at last decided to drive a much needed adit about 200 feet below the Old Men's Stage and this, Gilbert's Stage, was begun in 1798. The work can be inspected today and the quantity of spoil alone shows that the 220 yards to the Grand Pipe was no small undertaking. For example it was to be twenty-seven years before a project of similar magnitude was carried out at the Coniston copper mine when John Taylor began his Deep Level adit to the Bonsor Vein.

So in 1800 the lower part of the Grand Pipe was at last de-watered. This development heralded a new phase in the mine's working methods because internal connections eventually enabled wad from different parts of the mine to be trammed out by this new route. A substantial building was constructed at the entrance with a room where the workers changed their clothes under the eyes of a resident security guard. Three years later the efforts were rewarded with the discovery of a very large deposit of wad, Dixon's Pipe, which surprisingly had eluded the miners until now. This was found beyond the Grand Pipe "after a tedious search" and yielded five-hundred casks of the best wad containing about 140 lbs each. According to Postlethwaite working costs for 1803 only amounted to four percent of the profit for that year, but it must be remembered that a considerable amount of dead work had already been carried out. Today the dripping cavity of Dixon's Pipe, over 150 feet deep, lies empty and threatening far within the mine and clearly its working would have been severely handicapped without the drainage, ventilation and tramming capability provided by Gilbert's Stage. Nothing of this magnitude was ever found again but further exploration revealed Winkle's Pipe at the junction of two veins in 1812, which yielded eighty-seven casks of the best wad, now at 35s per pound, and a considerable amount of inferior wad.

These discoveries must have been a great relief to all concerned. By now the Keswick pencil makers were beginning to set up factories, including Jacob Banks, but it is ironic that by the time the firm of Banks and Co was established at Forge Mill in 1832 the wad mines were on the decline. According to Otley the price of best wad stood at 45s per pound in 1833, when a few casks were filled. To speed up exploration work it had become the practice to employ more hands and open the mine more frequently or for longer periods. Since the discovery of Winkle's Pipe a few encouraging deposits had been found including Grisdale's Pipe but there was nothing of great significance. And now the fortunes of the wad mine were further dampened by a backlash from the Napoleonic Wars. In 1795, after trade between Britain and France had ceased and the French were unable to obtain graphite of pencil quality, Napoleon appointed one of his army officers, Nicholas Jacques Conte, to experiment with artificial "leads" by mixing powdered graphite with powdered clay. The invention was a great success allowing pencils of different hardnesses to be manufactured. From about the mid 1830s the pencil industry turned more and more to composite graphite of this type and the demand for the pure wad diminished, although a stock was kept for the very best pencils.

From the late 1830s the mine was let to a series of companies and by 1850 a lower trial level, Robson's, had been driven on Rake Vein, for some years, and a crosscut had intersected Hasting's Pipe which had been worked to 100 feet below Gilbert's Stage but was waterlogged. In 1859 John Dixon was convinced there were "many sops or bodies of wad yet undiscovered", but apart from a possible isolated find in 1875 his hopes were never realised and when the last of the companies went into liquidation in 1891 the mines were abandoned for good. Towards the end of the century the pencil works were still drawing on their stocks of best wad but by 1906 foreign imports had completely taken over and sadly the story of Borrowdale wad came to an end.

One of the several marker stones that determined the boundary of the John Bankes lands. Unfortunately the vandals have been at work in recent times and one stone has been remade.
(photo, Dave Bridge)

Driven by muscle, sweat, and probably blood and a few tears, the coffin level of the Old Men's Stage meanders into the fell towards the Grand Pipe. As well as hammers and wedges, the old men used fire as a means of cracking the rock. Brushwood was heaped against the face and burned till the rock became hot. Then a mixture of water and vinegar was applied, causing the rock to splinter. *(photo, Dave Bridge)*

Things have changed in Borrowdale. Once the Wad Mines were visible from the surrounding fells but now the lower levels are cloaked in woodland. Here, looking east from the portal of Robson's Stage, the view is obscured by fir trees growing from the waste rock of the spoil heap. *(photo, Dave Bridge)*

The walls of the guard house outside the portal of Gilbert's Stage stand like a sentinel - after a century of abandonment. Many the poor miner who passed through the doorway under the watchful eye of the management. Many the wad pickers' lantern that flickered at night as the wind blew over the dark spoil heaps.
(photo, Dave Bridge)

SLATE

by Alastair Cameron

Lake District slate is 450 million years old. It was formed during the Ordovician era from volcanic dust and ash. It can be split or "cleaved" into sheets a few millimetres thick and has great resistance to climatic conditions. It is inert to virtually every form of chemical attack and is considered to be much superior to slate from other parts of Europe. It can be polished to give a beautiful finish and has become one of the most prized decorative building materials available.

It's impossible to say when quarrying for slate first took place but the indications are that it began in prehistoric times. Early man would have been aware of the sites where slate outcropped to the surface. He would have known of the special qualities of this rather unusual rock.

At a later period the Romans were familiar with the material and used it on their buildings. Later still, many of the monasteries and abbeys in the region were roofed with "well dressed" Lake District slate. Unfortunately, any form of documentation of these early slate workings is virtually non-existent. We can only surmise as to how the early years of the industry developed.

The first records that exist are from medieval times. There is a reference to a slate quarry being worked at Sadgill in Longsleddale in 1283 and a suggestion that some working of slate was taking place in Kirkby-in-Furness in the 1400s. It is very likely that, as with ore mining, the skills and crafts were imported from the continent to help establish the industry.

By the 1600s, with records at last available and accurate, the industry was already well developed. Workings in the Longsleddale and Kentmere areas were in steady production. So too were many of the Coniston quarries. By the early 1700s the Honister quarries were also well established. Records from this period also show that slate was being mined as well as quarried. Using techniques adapted from the ore mining industries, prospectors were driving tunnels or levels into the hillside to find richer deposits of slate deeper underground.

Future prosperity of workings would depend on three criteria: the amount of workable slate present, the quality of the slate, and the ease of transporting the finished product from the working site to where it was required.

Many of the enterprises were to fail because of the last of the three. During medieval times workings were usually started at the points of outcrop, where slate was visible at the surface. As these sites were frequently in very remote places, high on the fellside above the head of the dale, slate could only be transported by pack pony. Much of the road system had not been established and unless quarrymen constructed their own access roads, the workings would not develop further than providing slate for local need.

The boom in the slate industry came about as a result of the industrial revolution. During the 1800s those locations where transport problems could be overcome developed rapidly in size, providing materials to roof the houses of the expanding communities of northern England.

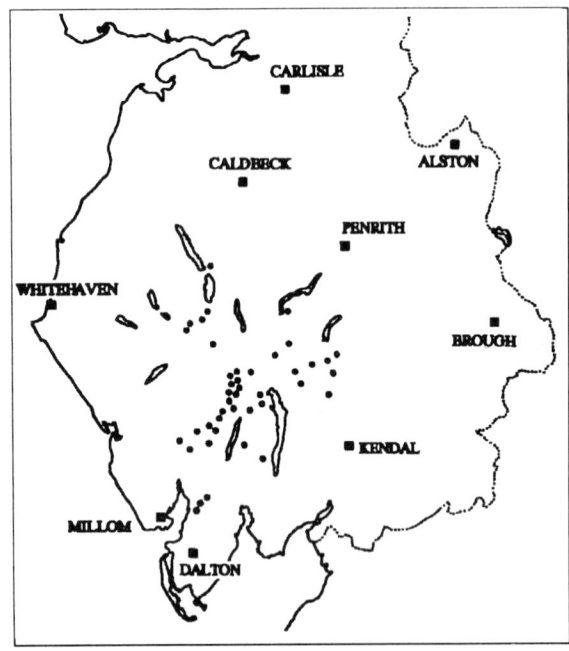

The general disposition of slate workings in Cumbria

In the eastern fells, Wrengill and Mosedale quarries became extensive despite their very remote locations. A cart road was constructed from the workings along the Longsleddale valley. After a lengthy journey, slate eventually arrived at the terminus of the Lancaster Canal, at Kendal, to be transported away. The nearby quarries at Kentmere also expanded and slate was carried by a similar route. Strictly speaking, the Kentmere workings were slate mines rather than quarries.

Coniston was to become a major centre for the industry. The extensive slate mines and quarries at Tilberthwaite and around Coniston Old Man had their own transport problems. Carts and sledges were used to take dressed slate from the workings down to Coniston village. Before the railway reached Coniston in 1859, slate was carted to Waterhead, taken in boats down Coniston Lake to Nibthwaite, and finally by cart to the port of Greenodd.

The Walna Scar quarries above the Duddon valley became extremely productive and slate was carried directly to the coast at Angerton, near Kirkby, via Broughton Mills. The massive Kirkby quarries were reputed to be the largest in England. They also used Angerton as an outlet until the Ulverston Canal opened in 1796. Later, with the opening of the Furness Railway through Kirkby in 1846, product was removed directly by rail. An inclined tramway was built from the quarry down to the railway at Sandside.

The workings at Honister faced major transport problems. Before 1800 most of the finished slate was taken away along a high level packhorse route known as Moses Trod, over the shoulders of some of Lakeland's highest mountains. The route ran to Wasdale Head and then on to the port of Ravenglass. Later, as Lakeland roads improved, it was possible to carry slate from the top of Honister Hause by horse and cart. But getting the slate down from the workings on the face of Honister Crag to the Hause was another story!

During the 18th century a number of fundamental changes took place in the industry. Gunpowder was being produced locally in about 1770. By 1800 it was in sufficient supply to make it available for slate quarrying and mining. The speed at which levels could be driven and faces worked with the aid of gunpowder could not be compared with the pre-gunpowder age.

Another change took place about a hundred years later. Before about 1890 roofing slates were produced at the site of extraction in stone cabins on the quarry floor or beside the entrance to the tunnels leading into the underground mining areas. At Honister, and at a number of other locations, slate was even dressed underground. The only material to be taken from the quarry or mine was finished roofing slates. All the waste spoil was left where it was discarded. With the introduction of electrically powered saws and more robust means of transport, it was possible to carry large slate blocks away from the quarry and work them in purpose built sheds, in much improved conditions. Eventually this was to become the normal method of operation in Lakeland quarries and mines.

A further innovation was the air-powered drill which was introduced in the early years of the 20th century. The powered drill replaced the traditional laborious hand-drilling methods for producing shot-holes, into which black-powder charges were placed. The rate at which levels could be extended and faces worked, when drills were used, was quite dramatic!

At the outbreak of the Great War many skilled slate workers were called to serve the country. It was with great reluctance that those who survived returned to the rough conditions of an industry such as slate mining. In a world of rapidly changing attitudes and standards, the working conditions in other industries became far more attractive.

By the end of the 1920s the Mosedale and Wrengill slate quarries in the Kentmere area had ceased production. So too had a number of workings at Coniston, including Walna Scar and Cove. But despite this, the industry in general was in good shape and survived the years of depression well. As some sites were closing others were expanding. At Honister slate mines a number of exploratory tunnels were driven to develop workings on new slate bands. At Torver, near Coniston, prospectors were busy on the high fells above the village. Claude Cann, a Cornish mining engineer, along with two companions, was trying to locate a rich area of slate. He was having very little success and was running out of money. Local opinion was sceptical. It was when his funds were virtually exhausted, and he was on the point of abandoning the project, that the level he was driving struck the huge deposit of green slate that subsequently became the Broughton Moor Quarry.

During the 1930s and 1940s the industry began to consolidate into a relatively few areas of operation, managed by a few proprietors. Slate extraction now concentrated on the areas of Honister, Kirkstone, Langdale, Coniston and Kirkby-in-Furness. The Buttermere Green Slate Company, who owned the Honister and surrounding slate mines, also acquired workings at Tilberthwaite, near Coniston, and at Elterwater in Langdale. All these remote slate quarries and mines were subsequently closed or sold. In the 1930s the Dubbs and Rigg Head slate mines in the Honister area were also closed. This left only the Honister workings themselves and the adjacent Yew Crag slate mines still operating.

By the 1940s all the workings in the eastern part of the Lake District had closed with the exception of the Kirkstone quarries, which are still operating today. Mandalls Slate Company worked the extensive Old Man quarries above Coniston as well as the nearby Blue Quarry, which closed during the Second World War. The Lakeland Green Slate and Stone Company operated at Moss Rigg and Hodge Close, in Tilberthwaite, a few miles north of Coniston.

In less than three years a number of major changes were to take place in Coniston. In 1962 the railway to Coniston closed and in 1960 Mandalls ceased operation at the Old Man workings. Fortunately for the village, a year earlier, the Lakeland Green Slate and Stone Company reopened a small working at Brossen Stone high on the east side of Coniston Old Man. Brossen Stone became a very extensive slate working, despite a difficult route of transport down to the village, and survives today.

The Broughton Moor workings to the south of Coniston also expanded considerably during this period as did the Burlington Slate Quarries at Kirkby-in-Furness. Eventually these two operations, as well as Mandalls and the Lakeland Green Slate and Stone Company, merged to operate under the one name of Burlington Slate Limited.

After the Second World War there was a noticeable increase in the use of heavy machinery in the quarries - boring rigs, face shovels, and heavy trucks replaced the old ways, and in a financially concerned environment created an economy of a scale that could not be ignored. To a great extent this was to mark the end of underground slate mining. Boring rigs could rip through the rock, massive explosive charges could be laid, and huge face shovels remove slate clogs with ease. It was no longer necessary to dig tunnels to seek deep bands of slate and then mine it in underground caverns. Modern machinery and techniques could remove hundreds of feet of overburden and allow deposits of slate to be worked as open quarries.

It was inevitable that such techniques would not go unnoticed by tourists and environmental groups. From 1960 to the present day many battles have been fought in the courts and at public inquiries.

Not only were methods of operation changing but so were the markets. The building construction industry now favours light weight synthetic materials for cladding house roofs - slate is used only in special circumstances. But new markets have opened up and there is still a world wide and expanding demand for Lakeland slate in the field of decorative cladding.

Slate is both attractive and very durable and has now been used for the cladding of many prestige buildings round the world. Its resistance to acid corrosion and other forms of attack make it very attractive to designers. New computer aided technology has been developed and slate is cut to very tight tolerances prior to packing and shipping to destinations in Japan, Saudi Arabia, and the United States.

Uses are also being found for the large quantities of waste rock which accumulate on spoil tips. The development of modern and powerful crushing machines has meant that slate rock can be converted into a valuable commodity in the form of in-fill and foundation for roads and buildings, replacing limestone and gravel.

New methods of extraction are also constantly being developed. The relatively new technique of diamond-wire sawing involves cutting through rock with a diamond studded wire in a similar way to slicing cheese with a cheese-wire. The result is that far less slate is lost through damage by blasting with powder.

All this is very far removed from the days when Sammy Burns sat on his low stool cleaving slate by hand in an underground cavern at Honister at the turn of the century.

In 1985 the Honister slate workings closed. Had it not been for the reopening of a small underground working at Tilberthwaite by George Tar, of Coniston, in the same year, slate mining in Lakeland would have ceased at that point. The Tilberthwaite working continues to prosper, as do two other private ventures nearby, namely the High Fellside Quarry and a small operation at Hodge Close.

In 1989 Burlington Slate closed their offices at Coniston and transferred all administration to Kirkby-in-Furness, outside the National Park. However, Brossen Stone and Low Brandy Crag quarries are still operating at Coniston, as are Broughton Moor to the south and Spout Crag and Elterwater quarries at Langdale. Rough blocks of slate are now transported from the various quarries to Kirkby-in-Furness for processing. The independent Kirkstone Green Slate Quarries extract slate from their site above Kirkstone Pass and transport it to Skelwith Bridge for processing.

The industry is now only a fraction of the size it was at the turn of the century. Those who walk the Lakeland fells frequently come across remains of old slate mines and quarries, a silent reminder of a once extensive industry. Over the years the workings have blended in well with the surroundings and are usually unobtrusive. Many of the valley workings have disappeared under a blanket of birch shrub.

For some time industrial archaeologists with an interest in old mine workings have studied the remains, both on the surface and underground. The lives of the quarrymen and the history of their communities is closely connected with that of the slate workings. Villages such as Coniston, Rosthwaite, Elterwater, and Torver, are quarrying villages which have developed over several centuries to meet the needs of the industry.

Workings in the Coniston area have been studied extensively. In the early years of this century the total workforce at the quarries on Coniston Old Man, and at Moss Rigg and Hodge Close, amounted to several hundred men and boys. Between 1870 and 1900 the workforce in the Coniston copper mine was declining. It was fortunate that alternative employment existed in the slate industry.

There are extensive underground workings within Coniston Old Man, from an altitude of about 1200 feet to just below the summit. The spoil tips and the former entrances are to be found on the east shoulder of the mountain. The lower entrances are now blocked but those of the upper workings, at Saddlestone, have been explored in recent times. Formerly, these workings were separate and consisted of levels taken in from the surface for some distance into the hill until good slate "metal" was reached. As slate was removed, a sizeable cavern was left. More extensive workings during the last fifty years have caused many of the caverns to break into each other to form enormous open voids. One particular void has formed at the Moss Head and Spion Kop workings. Walkers climbing Coniston Old Man by the "tourist" route would be amazed to learn of the cavity beneath their feet.

During the 1880s slate from these high workings was taken down to Coniston village by horse-drawn sledge. In 1903 an aerial ropeway was commissioned from the workings to the road head and from then until the workings closed, in 1960, this became the main means of bringing slate down. The remains of the various ropeways can still be seen on the Old Man.

Another area which has received the attention of industrial archaeologists is the Honister slate workings at the head of the Borrowdale valley. The main area of extraction was inside Honister Crag and also at Yew Crag on the other side of the pass. Prior to the 1880s all "dressed" slate was sledged by hand down the gullies and screes of Honister Crag. By 1897 an external incline had been constructed up the face of the crag and this allowed much more efficient removal of slate from the underground workings. Much of the incline remains and is considered to be one of the finest monuments to Victorian engineering in Cumbria.

In the 1920s two further inclines were constructed inside the crag to allow larger blocks of slate to be removed for working in the newly-constructed cutting sheds at Honister Hause. From the foot of the incline, slate blocks were brought out onto the surface of the crag and carried to the Hause by aerial ropeway.

An external incline was also constructed at Yew Crag and this remained in operation, albeit with various modifications, until the Yew Crag workings closed in 1966.

There is still much more for the industrial archaeologist to interpret in the slate workings of Lakeland.

Although the industry is surviving well in Cumbria, environmental concerns are constantly voiced about the visual effect of some present-day workings such as Brossen Stone and Low Brandy Crag at Coniston. It would be a tragedy if lack of foresight and moderation by the quarry operators caused this traditional industry to die because of environmental pressure.

Honister Crag, taken from the northern slope of Dale Head, about 1910. The causeway skirting the fell to the foot of the crag was known as the Monkey Shelf, and was used to bring slate clogs from the incline terminus. The incline was operated by gravity, the weight of the laden trolleys descending being sufficient to haul unladen trolleys to the top. Formed in three independent sections (Ash Gill, Nag Back, and Bull Gill at the lower end), slate from the Honister Vein was conveyed from the closeheads inside Fleetwith Pike, down the crag, to the processing sheds - till the incline was superseded by other methods. The lower portions have been swept away by waste tossed from the closeheads on the Kimberley Vein. *(photo, Abraham of Keswick)*

Ropeway terminus, situated halfway down the old Bull Gill Incline. The ropeway, installed by Whites of Widnes in 1927, superseded the incline but was itself superseded by the blasting of the Link Level, a tunnel connecting the terminus with the workings on the Kimberley Vein. From the 1960s, till the cessation of work on the Honister Vein, clogs were lowered down the rails, from the head of the ropeway, to the Link Level portal, a few feet below, and trammed directly to the sheds on Honister Hause. *(photo, Alastair Cameron)*

The internal incline on the Honister Vein. Installed during the 1920s, the internal incline replaced the old external inclines of Honister Crag, which were affected by the atrocious Lakeland winters. Slate was lowered from the closehead galleries on trolleys capable of carrying a "clog wagon" laden with slate. The empties were returned to the head of the incline by a counter weight descending on the inner set of the four rails in the picture. The counter weight was made of cast iron, and low enough to pass beneath the trolley as the two components passed in the centre of the incline. The internal incline worked in conjunction with the compressed-air ropeway on the old Bull Gill Incline, and was installed at about the same time. *(photo, Alastair Cameron)*

The carrier trolley, still in position on the internal incline of Honister Crag. The turntable on the trolley top allowed clog wagons to be run on from the piers of the various levels, then slewed through 90° to be off-loaded at the bottom.

The counter weight, still under tension on its steel cable. The weight was designed to pass beneath the carrier trolley when meeting midway on the incline.
(photos, Alastair Cameron)

At the head of the internal incline stands the brake house, complete with corrugated zinc roof, brake drum, and indicator clock. From here the operator was able to control the rate of descent of the laden trolleys. From the position of the dial on the indicator he could determine the position of the trolley in the darkness of the incline. *(photo, Alastair Cameron)*

Illustrating one of the many dangers of underground quarrying, a razor-sharp flake of Honister slate bridges the tramway. The right-hand wall is constructed of "muck" - the corners docked from slate clogs. Underground buttresses constructed of waste are a common feature in the Cumbrian closeheads. They serve the dual purpose of providing an inexpensive means of controlling the waste while supporting the workings at the same time.
(photo, Ian Matheson)

The slate closeheads of the Honister mines are, in themselves, monuments to the quarrymen who worked them. These dark voids once echoed to the blast of black-powder and dynamite - but now they are silent and will probably remain so. Note the stone walls on the left of the picture and the hundreds of tons of "muck" heaped up behind. Tramlines run off through a stone-arched level towards the internal incline of the Honister Vein, while on the right the closehead descends to a lower working horizon. The smooth wall on the extreme right of the picture is formed by the "bate", the natural cleavage plane of the slate. This differs from the bedding plane by a few degrees only. Two stratifications of bedding plane can be seen in the bottom right of the picture, ascending at a slightly shallower angle to that of the bate.   *(photo, Ian Matheson)*

Test boreholes in the slate rock of the Honister Vein, an attempt to discover fresh beds of slate metal during the 1980s by the then proprietors, the Welsh quarrying company, McAlpines of Penrhyn.   *(photo, Alastair Cameron)*

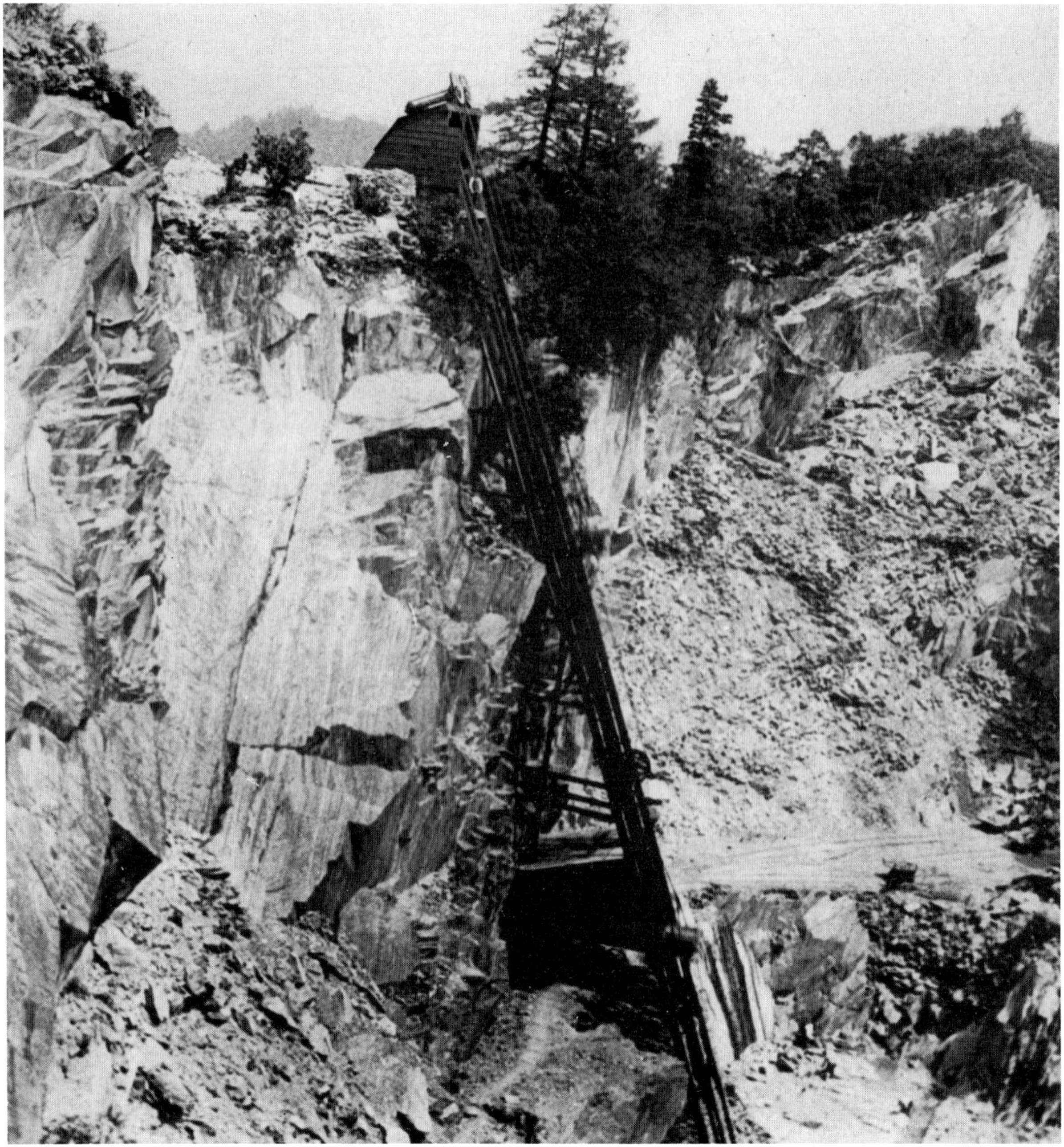

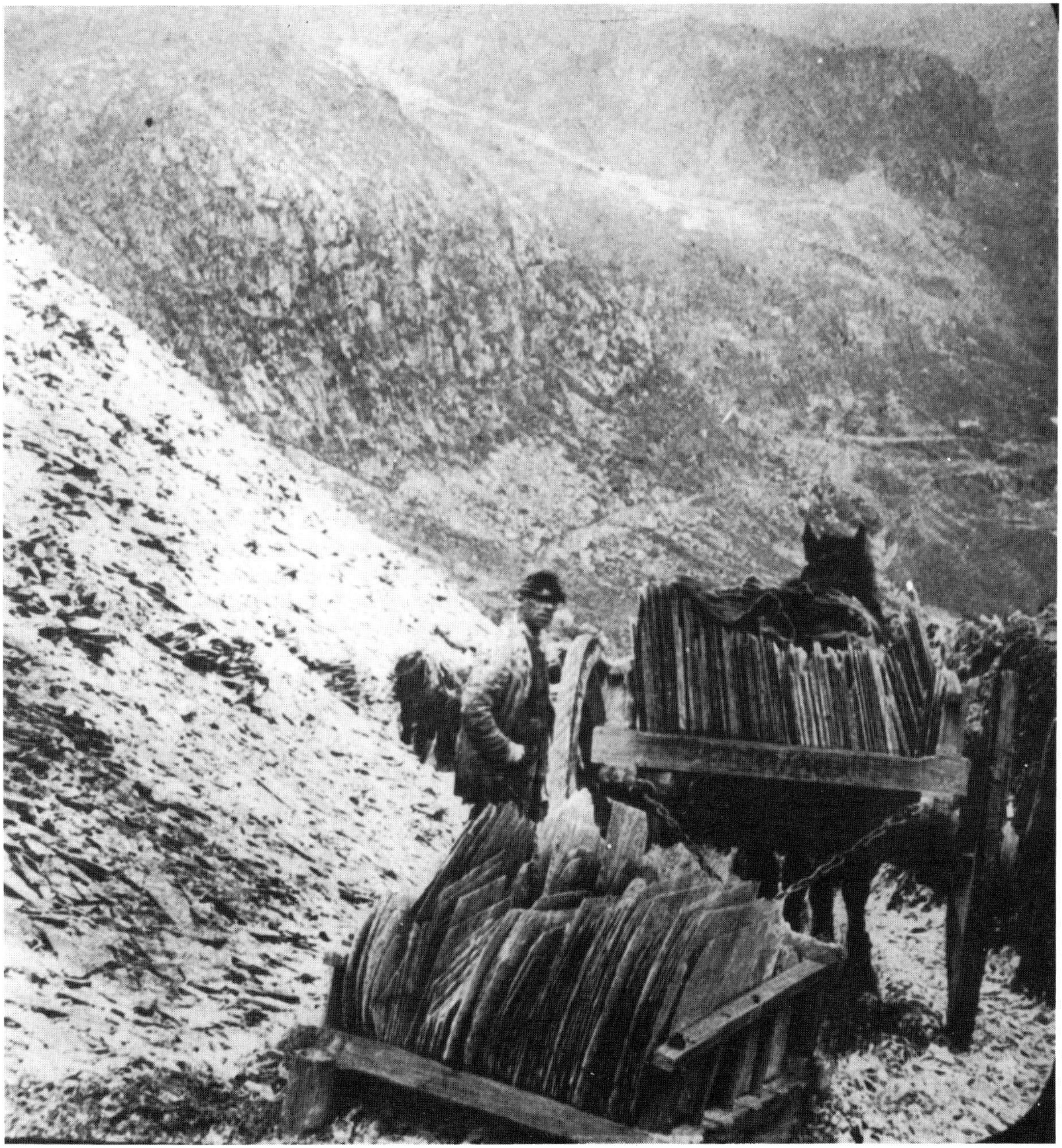

Overleaf: Hodge Close Quarry, near Tilberthwaite Gill, about 1900. Gravity was one of the main workhorses of the 19th and 20th century quarrymen. Gravity inclines became more and more elaborate as engineering skills progressed - but not only was gravity used to lower slate bogies to the processing sheds (usually situated beneath the quarries) - it was also used for raising slate from the depths. At Hodge Close, and at the Burlington Quarries at Kirkby-in-Furness, water balances were employed to great effect. The balances worked on the principle that a heavy tank of water descending on one set of guides was sufficient to raise a bogey and slate clog, to which it was attached by means of a cable and pulley system, to a predetermined height. Once off-loaded at the top of the water balance, the tank (which was then positioned at the foot) was drained and became the lighter of the two components. The weight of the empty trolley at the top was then sufficient to lift the empty tank back up the guides. At Hodge Close the slate was raised to a point midway up the quarry face, from where it was run off into a level and trammed out to day. Although the quarry is now flooded and the water balance long gone, it is still possible to walk through the level and stand at the point where the slate was off-loaded.

Overleaf: Carting silver-grey slate from the Old Man Quarries at Coniston. The track from the quarry bank on the Old Man was steep and winding, so sledges were used as in other parts of the Lakes. Not only could double the amount of slate be carted by each horse, the sledges also acted as brakes on the severe gradients. It is interesting to note that although the tracks were cobbled with slate off-cuts to provide a substantial foundation, when the quarries were in operation the tracks were covered in a superficial layer of "rivings", the waste chips from the processing sheds, to prevent the sledges careering away and provide a smooth surface on which to run. In the far distance can be seen the miners' track descending from the copper mines at Levers Water, and the sheds at Paddy End Mine.

Opposite: Beneath the tips of Hodge Close Quarry, rivers and dressers at work in an open-fronted shed. Quarrymen worked in "companies", groups of workers who would set a bargain with the quarry agent to work a particular section of the face. They were then paid a predetermined sum for the tonnage of finished slate they produced, the price depending on the quality of the rock in the face and the amount of "crag", or "muck", that would have to be disposed of. Companies varied depending on locality but the typical arrangement would consist of two rockhands, who worked the face, two rivers, for docking the clogs and splitting the slate to the required thickness, and a dresser who trimmed the slates to the final size and shape. In the picture the river on the right is splitting the slate with a mallet and chisel - a method introduced from North Wales at the turn of the century. The two men on the left are using the traditional Lakeland riving hammers, a method which required a great deal more skill. The gentleman seated on the floor is the dresser, trimming the slates with his whittle and brake. The large wooden mallets in the foreground are known as mells - used for docking the slate clogs to a size suitable for riving purposes.

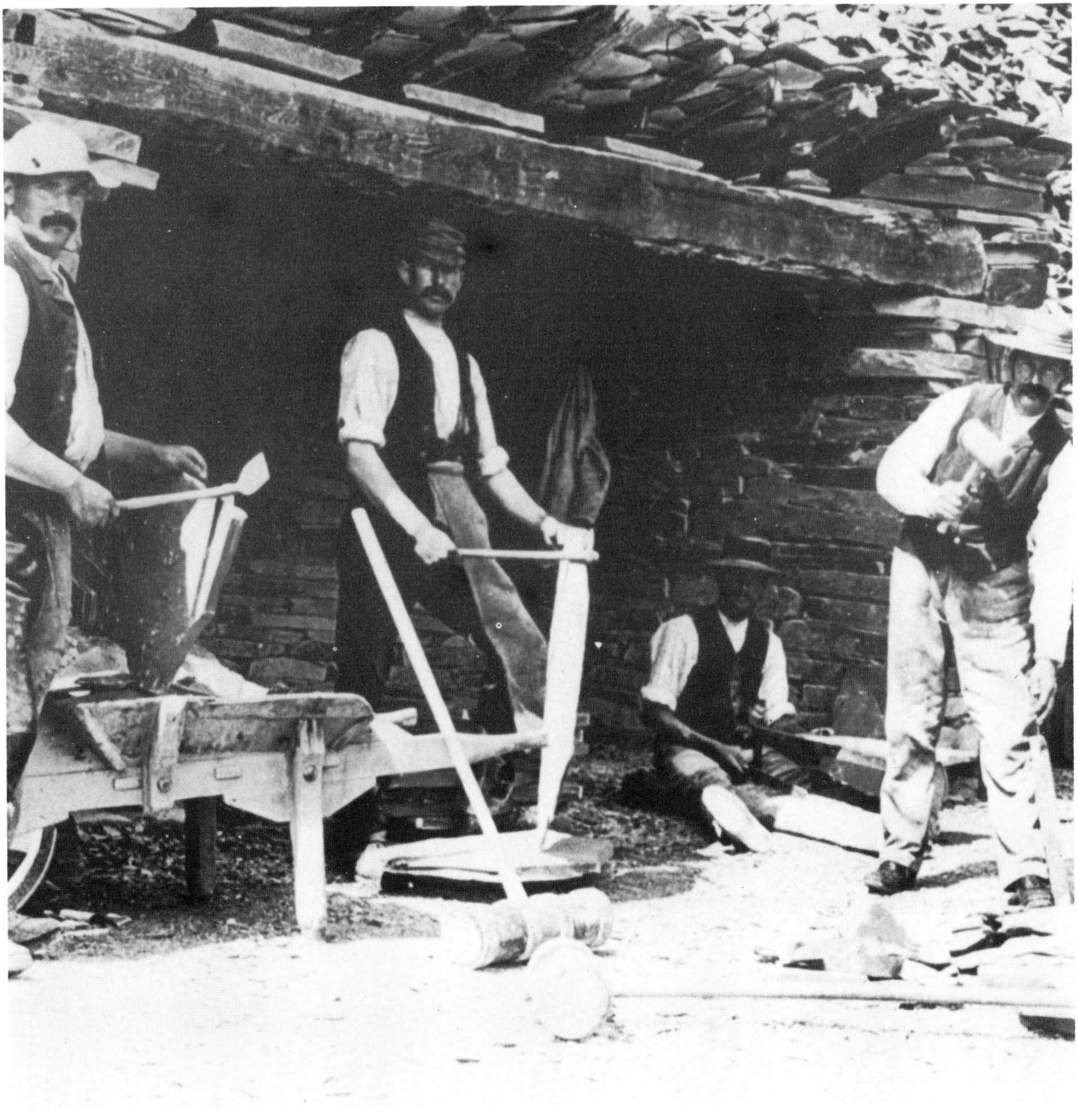

The saw shed of Spion Kop, one of the highest quarries on Coniston Old Man, stands perched on the edge of the quarry tip overlooking the Bonsor dressing floors in Coppermines Valley. Named after a British defeat in the Boer War, the quarry was the highest closehead in the colossal Saddlestone and Moss Head complex of workings which virtually ripped the heart out of the mountain. Only the ancient Scald Cop and Low Water quarries are higher. One of the first electric stone saws to be used in the slate quarrying industry was located at this site, finished roofing slates and walling stone being lowered over a thousand feet, to the foot of the fell, on an aerial ropeway installed in 1902. *(photo, Alen McFadzean)*

On the bank at Saddlestone Quarry, the ruins of Mandall's saw shed and office overlook Coniston and the eastern slopes of Wetherlam. The saw shed housed a fixed-height utility circular saw, purchased from the Bramley Engineering Company of Leeds in 1938. The last of the big ropeways was installed during the same year by Whites of Widnes. The terminus pylon is still visible in the centre of the picture. Slate clogs were lowered down the mountain from the top and middle levels of Moss Head Quarry, while clogs from the higher levels of Saddlestone descended on a separate ropeway, the anchor bars of which can be seen embedded in concrete immediately in front of the office. Slate production came to an end on the Old Man's silver-grey vein in the late 1950s, but resumed again in 1982 with the reopening of Low Brandy Crag Quarry at Paddy End. *(photo, Alastair Cameron)*

If gravity was the main source of motive power in the Cumbrian slate industry, water came a close second. The power for the Saddlestone saw, the air-compressors, and the drilling equipment in the blacksmith's shop, came from a pelton wheel situated in the power house at Brandy Crag Quarry. Water descended under pressure from Low Water tarn in a cast iron pipe, only sections of which remain. The power house, several hundred feet below the banks of the tarn, is devoid of its roof but has recently been rescued from destruction by the Cumbria Amenity Trust.
(photo, Alastair Cameron)

One small corner of the colossal Moss Head complex of workings, deep in the heart of the Old Man. To the left of the picture the floor plunges fifty feet to the Moss Head Low Level, while above the figure in the centre the walls rise sheer through the worked-out floor of the Moss Head Top Level to the roof of Spion Kop, over a hundred feet above. The rock wall on the left is a gigantic pillar of slate, left in situ to support the roof. The smooth wall on the right is a "slipe", a natural division in the slate rock, usually composed of inferior material.
(photo, Alastair Cameron)

Cathedral Cavern, part of the Little Langdale Quarries in the heart of the Lake District. Here the roof of the closehead is supported by a fifty foot pillar of slate, left in position by the old men. Note the "cross-holes" near the base of the pillar, holes bored *across* the bate in order to cut the rock from the face. Not all Lakeland slate can be quarried in this manner. The blue-grey of Kirkby-in-Furness will burst into fragments when blasted with cross-holes. Only "bate-holes", holes bored along the plane of the cleavage, can be used to slice the metal from the quarry face. *(photo, J & E Forder)*

Named after the quarryman who designed them, a Matt Spedding tunnel runs beneath the underground tips in one of the Hodge Close closeheads. The tunnels were composed of slate waste, built up in walls, then topped with a flag roof. These tunnels can be found in many Lakeland quarries, both underground and running through the surface tips. *(Alastair Cameron)*

A quarryman's hut, built completely of slate, high in the fells above Tilberthwaite. Huts, or cabins, like this were once a familiar sight in the Lakeland fells and provided a refuge from the harsh mountain weather.   *(photo, Peter Fleming)*

An open-fronted riving shed stands at the entrance to a small closehead in the fells above Tilberthwaite. At one time, when the slate industry was at its zenith, hundreds of similar sheds were built in the valley bottoms and on the high fells, depending where the slate veins were running. This is thought to be the last open-fronted shed in the Lakes to be standing complete with roof - a situation that will not last for long, judging the state of the timbers. *(photo, Peter Fleming)*

Walna Scar Quarries on the fells above Seathwaite, Dunnerdale, were famous for their beautifully banded slates. The bands denote the beds, or layers, of deposition, formed as the rock was laid as dust and detritus in water. The layers bear no relation to the "bate", the plane along which all slates cleave. The bate in the slab above is denoted by the upper surface plane and runs at right angles to the beds. *(photo, Anton & Sheila Thomas)*

Arch over a tramway running from a slate quarry adit at Walna Scar, Dunnerdale.
(photo, Anton & Sheila Thomas)

Natural "roundheads" - the local term for slates dressed in the traditional fashion - high in the Lakeland fells. Here the slate outcrops on the surface and has burst, either through the actions of severe frost or by the hand of 19th century man, to fall in perfectly cleaved slabs. The "bate", the cleavage inherent in all slates, can be discerned edge on, running at a steep angle through the "growing" rock.   *(photo, Peter Fleming)*

The Burlington Slate Quarries, Kirkby-in-Furness, June 1984. Three-hundred feet high from the top of the Backway to the floor of the Sink, these quarries have been worked continuously for several hundred years. Originally worked as separate entities, the quarries became a single concern during the 1840s when the mineral owner, the Earl of Burlington, cancelled the leases and laid the initial miles of track of the Furness Railway to his slate sidings at the foot of the moor. The main quarry, which is an amalgamation of Fisher, Smithy Hill, Town, Lord, and Hunter quarries, is now the largest slate quarry in England.
(photo, Alen McFadzean)

A quarry face below the East End in the Burlington Slate Quarries at Kirkby. The ledge on which the quarryman is standing is called a "foot", a free bedding plane from which the slate can be dislodged with little effort. The pale bands running at intervals of a few centimetres through the rock, and parallel with the feet, are also bedding planes but do not affect the structure of the slate. They do not form a plane of weakness and cannot be utilised in the riving process. The flat quarry floor is the result of wire-saw cutting, while the face has been worked by eight-foot bate-holes, several of which can be seen in the picture. The bate, the plane of cleavage, is running across the face and gives the rock the flat, slabby appearance. *(photo, Alen McFadzean)*

IRON

by Richard Hewer and Alen McFadzean

The iron industry has slowly matured within the Lake counties for centuries, with industrial growth spreading from the coastal plateau workings and the narrow veins of the fells to the huge mining and iron smelting complexes of the late 19th and 20th centuries. The industry declined during the mid 20th century because of dwindling ore reserves and the pressures of economic viability.

The mining areas were divided into well defined regions. Major deposits occurred around Egremont, Cleator, Cleator Moor, Ennerdale, Eskdale, Millom and Ulverston, with numerous smaller deposits within the Lakeland fells - for example Langdale, Coniston and Grasmere.

The Whitehaven region has evolved from several distinct groups of rock. The carboniferous limestone overlying the Skiddaw slate on the south-eastern side has in turn been overlaid by the coal measures in the north-west. The southern area is covered by the St Bees sandstone. The principal ore bodies occurred within the seven bands of the carboniferous limestone series, the latter having been subjected to varying degrees of earth movement and faulting whilst the iron solutions penetrated the fault lines from above and below. The resultant ore bodies formed large flats (bodies of solid ore) which connected with the bedding planes of the host rock, irregular bodies occurring as large swellings within the vein, or true veins or faults whereby the hematite solution followed the lines of weakness. The miners were forever optimists, for, just ahead of them, the vein could open out into a new and profitable shoot of ore.

Large, shallow deposits were extensively worked by the early miners. Development was rapid - easily worked deposits provided greater profits but with this ambitious drive came the dangers and disasters. Roof falls were commonplace; holing into abandoned workings and slides of disturbed ground were all part of the miners' way of life. In several instances, where all the ore had been removed from the flats, it was necessary to fill the large voids with waste rock and in some cases sand was blown into the cavities, leaving only heavily timbered shafts for access to the lower workings.

Several varieties of iron were mined. The most common type was compact, hard, massive and of a bluish-purple hue (hard blue) usually associated with the flats. Kidney or pencil ore was often found in irregular deposits in the 1st and 2nd limestones. Specular ore was something of a rarity, often found in cavities (loughs) and saved to be sold as specimens by the miners (a lucrative sideline). Lesser ores consisted of dark "black" soft ore; smit ore (very greasy and highly coloured); muck or "ring" ore.

Research and field work have shown that the deposits

were exploited from Roman times. Several bloomery sites suggest operations by early British or Norse settlers. Many of the sites date from the late medieval period but could have obliterated earlier workings. The earliest documented evidence of mining within Egremont parish relates to Bigrigg Mine in 1179. The surface cover was shallow and the deposits easily exploited, probably as opencasts. Between 1179 and 1635 the search for further deposits was intensified. During the later years a large, pure deposit of ore was discovered at Langhorn which, by 1709, when it was still being worked, had yielded over 21,500 tons of ore. As the miners searched for new deposits several ancient workings were discovered revealing wooden pumps, wooden spades and clay pipes. The workings could be dated between 1585 (introduction of tobacco) and 1602 when spades had metal tips fitted.

Advertisements often appeared in the local papers offering plots of land..."with great prospects of iron ore". In 1784 Crowgarth Mine tapped a particularly rich body of "hard blue" ore. 20,000 tons were transported to the Carron Foundry in Stirlingshire. After this date there followed a ten year slump in the iron trade which slowed development work in Cumbria. However, after this unsettled period the metal prices improved and mining gained momentum until the decline in the 20th century.

Exploration within the Lakeland fells was spasmodic. The veins of hematite were small, rich, but often mixed with stone. Transport was difficult and iron prices were low. During the early 1840s prospectors tried any likely veins but it wasn't until the mid 1860s and early 1870s that serious attempts to work the lodes were instigated. The valley sides of Ennerdale Water received considerable attention, especially at the sites of ancient workings. The Crag Fell Mine (Ennerdale No.2) was the only producer of ore of any quantity. Meanwhile, Floutern Tarn (Red Gill Mine) received notoriety for the activities in share dealing by Faithful Cookson who was also associated with several other ventures in the area and in neighbouring Eskdale. The trials around Scale Beck and along the flank of Gale Fell provided a limited amount of ore which was sorted, cleaned, bagged and wheelbarrowed away!

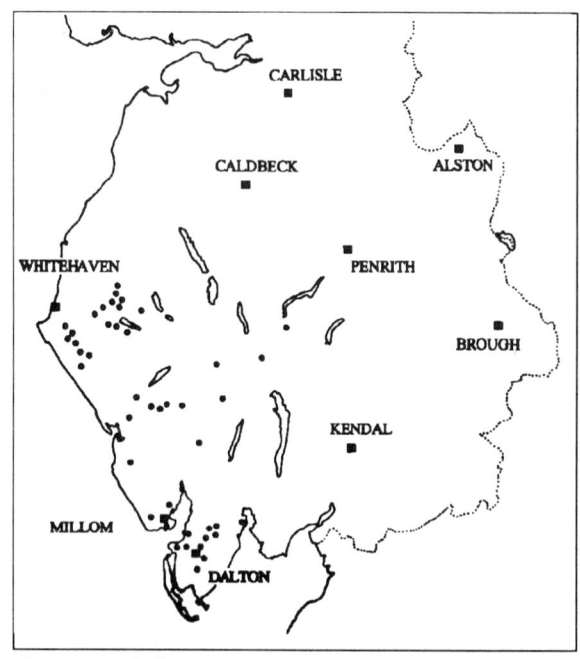

The general disposition of iron mines in Cumbria

The Kelton and Knockmurton mines were the only large producers of ore from the Skiddaw slate formation. The mines were owned by William Baird and Co, of Gartsherrie, Scotland, who had ventured south in search of quality ore for their blast furnaces. Between 1869 and 1913 over 1.25 million tons were raised, much of which was transported to their works, though some went to the Moss Bay and Harrington furnaces near Whitehaven and a little to the Midlands.

The mines of Eskdale have fortunately left us with the Ravenglass and Eskdale Railway. This was constructed solely to serve the mines and was nearly "lost" when the workings closed down. Nab Gill Mine, started in 1870 by Whitehaven Iron Mines Ltd, worked the veins in the Eskdale granite. It produced roughly 8,000 tons per annum; however, tonnages declined after 1881. Gill Force and Gate Crag mines on the south side of the valley were the second major producer, and were worked by the South Cumberland Iron Company. A branch line from the Ravenglass & Eskdale Railway served the latter workings. Several small workings dot the slopes of the valley (eg. Bann Garth and Christcliff). The iron ore was extracted by overhead stoping and removed from Nab Gill by way of an inclined tramway to the main line.

The upsurge in both coal and iron mining provided an impetus towards further development of the railway network. The small country lanes could not cope with the volume of traffic transporting ore to the ports and major rail headings. During the winter months the lanes became impassable, often deep in hematite slurry. Horses suffered leg and back injuries through falls and overloaded wagons. Prosecutions were brought against the owners by the RSPCA.

The railway companies quickly developed a programme of line expansion, welcomed by many but not all. 1845 saw the Maryport to Carlisle Railway and during the following year the Dalton to Kirkby line became operational. The Whitehaven to Ravenglass line opened in 1849 and was extended to Foxfield in 1850. By 1857 the Whitehaven to Egremont and Frizington line was completed. The line was extended to Marron in 1866 where it formed a junction with the Cockermouth and Penrith Railway. The Furness Railway Company constructed an extension from Egremont to Sellafield in 1869. Previously ores had to be shipped by sea from Whitehaven. 1875-76 saw the opening of the Ravenglass and Eskdale Railway with the Cleator and Workington Junction Railway in 1878

The railway companies, during the early 1870s, adjusted their carriage rates. Bairds, of Kelton and Knockmurton mines, were not happy with the new arrangements and approached the Cleator and Workington Junction Railway who agreed to build a connecting branch from Distington to Bairds' mineral railway at Rowrah. This line was known as Bairds Line and had gradients which were described as "ferocious".

The remains of mineral lines and branches still survive, silent, overgrown, and water-logged - cuttings full of refuse, bridges raided of their stones. Many led chequered lives, none moreso than the Ravenglass and Eskdale Railway which within seven months lost the traffic it was constructed for and yet, a hundred-and-fifteen years later, still survives.

The Rowrah and Kelton Fell mineral railway was surveyed as a simple branch line to Bairds' mines; however, the planned route aroused interest in possible extensions and alternatives towards the infant mining ventures in the fells. Various schemes were suggested, for example in 1871 an extension was envisaged from Knockmurton to Red Gill Mine (Floutern Tarn) where a stationary steam engine would raise the bogies of ore up an incline to the line. A variation of this plan adjusted the track from 3 ft to 2 ft gauge, double tracked and suitable for carrying bogies containing 12 cwts of ore each. Another suggestion included a tunnel a quarter of a mile in length.

A scheme suggesting a route from Cockermouth through the Vale of Lorton (passing the Scale Hill Hotel) by way of the Mosedale Beck valley and travelling along the flank of Gale Fell towards Scale Beck Mine, eleven miles and estimated at a cost of 120,000, met fierce local resistance which took the proposers by surprise. But not so, in 1881, when it was proposed to take a branch line from the Rowrah and Kelton Fell Railway at Kirkland down to the head of Ennerdale Water by way of a large bridge over Croasdale Beck. The aim was to tap the supply route from the iron mines in the Ennerdale valley.

The Rowrah and Kelton Fell line was approved and the other proposals were abandoned. How the Lakeland scene could have changed if all the schemes had materialised. The line became operational in 1877, serving the mines until 1913 and Kirkland village until 1927. One of the saddle tank locos still survives, built specifically for the line by Neilsons of Glasgow and named Kelton Fell. The engine can be seen at the Scottish Railway Preservation Society museum, Bo'nes Railway, Falkirk. The engine was built in 1876 and had a most eventful career.

Furness and Hodbarrow

The hematite ore field of Furness is bordered to the north by silurian slate and to the south by permo-triassic sandstone, the host rocks being a succession of six distinct limestones deposited during the Carboniferous period. Unlike the non-ferrous mineral veins of the nearby Lakeland mountains, the hematite lodes of Furness conform to no particular pattern. Only in certain instances - mainly in the southern and eastern areas of the ore field - do they manifest in true mineral vein form, the deposits of the north and west being in highly irregular masses.

Large scale mining has taken place at a number of locations between the towns of Barrow and Ulverston. The major ore deposits were situated at Askam, Roanhead, Park, Yarlside, Stank, Mouzell, Crossgates, Marton and Lindal; with peripheral deposits at Urswick, Stainton, Pennington, and Plumpton.

Across the Duddon estuary, in the carboniferous limestone between Millom and Haverigg, ore was mined at Hodbarrow from one of the largest bodies of hematite ever discovered. Three miles to the north-west, an outlying vein in the Wicham Valley yielded hematite ore from the fault between the limestone and the older Skiddaw slate.

Just when mining began is a point open to conjecture. Archaeological evidence determines that ore was smelted in the vicinity of Urswick during the Iron Age by indigenous Celts.

During the medieval period the economic structure of Furness was controlled by a handful of landed families and the Cistercian monks of the Abbey of Saint Mary. The monks commenced mining at a place called Orgrave, on the outskirts of Dalton, prior to 1235, and by 1300 had developed several locations for the winning of ore, mostly in the vicinity of Dalton. These initial ventures were probably opencast workings, exploiting shallow layers of mineral - worked with ease once the overlying boulder clay and pinnel had been removed.

In 1396, William de Merton bequeathed land surrounding the villages of Marton, Dalton, and Orgrave to the Abbot and Covenant of the Blessed Mary of Furness, so that the monks could "throw out and raise all manner of mineral or ore there found out of the mines". The wording suggests that techniques had changed, that the monks were, by this period, digging deeper and toiling in pits beneath the earth.

The smelting of the hematite was achieved using methods similar to the crude techniques employed by the ancient Celts. Ore was heated in primitive hearths called bloomeries - small clay domes in which charcoal burnt to a temperature sufficient to render the ore malleable, or soft enough to allow the impurities to be beaten out by the forgeman. The abundance of suitable woodland for the provision of charcoal, rather than the proximity of hematite, usually dictated the siting of the bloomeries. It was not uncommon for ore to be transported to the banks of Coniston Water (along Iron Yeat) during the monastic period, and smelted where both charcoal and water were plentiful.

Towards the close of the monastic period this traditional mode of smelting was superseded by the stringheath, a slightly larger version of the bloomery but with the addition of a bellows mechanism powered by a waterwheel. A further refinement was the bloomsmithy, where the waterwheel powered a mechanical forge hammer as well as applying the blast to the hearth. The 17th century saw the gradual domination of the bloomsmithy as the main means of converting raw hematite into marketable wrought iron. But it was the introduction of the charcoal blast furnace to the valleys of south Cumbria which revolutionised the process and stimulated local mining into a vigorous and highly competitive industry.

The first charcoal blast furnace was built at Cunsey in 1711, close to the shores of Windermere, by a group of Cheshire businessmen. The local ironmasters reacted with remarkable celerity and during the same year erected a furnace at Backbarrow, on the river Leven. Such was the impact of these two smelters on the local economy, that within forty years a number of similar furnaces had sprung up at Leighton, near Carnforth, Duddon Bridge, near Broughton-in-Furness, Nibthwaite, at the foot of Coniston Water, Lowwood, on the banks of the Leven, Newland, near Ulverston, and Pennybridge, on the river Crake. The success of the ironmasters is put into perspective, along with the rate at which the iron industry - as a whole - expanded, by the fact that several charcoal blast furnaces were established in the north of Scotland - where charcoal was plentiful - to which Furness hematite was shipped for processing.

The iron industry was further stimulated by the introduction of more advanced smelting and refining techniques during the 19th century, but the main boost - Furness' introduction to the industrial revolution - occurred in 1711 on the wooded banks of England's largest lake.

Alongside these developments in smelting, a similar pattern in mine ownership began to emerge. With the gradual adoption of the stringheath and the bloomsmithy came the farmer entrepreneurs and the landed ironmasters, filling the vacuum left by the monks. Mining methods were crude, development restricted to narrow strip fields and complex field boundaries. And with the charcoal blast furnaces came the mining companies, organised bodies of local men and outsiders looking for opportunities in a land rich and red with iron ore. By the mid 19th century the ore fields had been apportioned into definitive mining royalties leased by a variety of companies, some retaining their traditional landed roots, others captained by experts trained in the hard-rock mines of Cornwall.

John Bolton, author of *Geological Fragments of Furness and Cartmel*, gives us a unique insight into the cramped though incredibly industrious mines around Dalton in 1869.

This hill [High Haume] is a favourable site for a view of the surrounding district, and before we descend let us examine some of its physical features. Before us is the real California of Britain - the great hematite iron ore district of Furness - some of the principal mines forming a semicircle at the base of the hill. Commencing our review at the north-west, we have first, the new mines of Messrs Kennedy Brothers, on the Askam estate; almost adjoining these the splendid mines of Messrs Schneider, Hannay, and Co (this firm has now become the Barrow Hematite Iron and Steel and Mining Co), at Park; close to which are the Ronhead mines of Kennedy Brothers. Glancing round the foot of the hill we find Elliscales, Messrs Ashburner and Son; Butts Beck, Ricket Hills, Cross Gates, J. Rawlinson Esq; the Ure Pits, Ulverston Mining Company; Mousell Mines, Messrs Schneider, Hannay, and Co; all skirting the base of High Haume, and constituting a circle arc of 180 degrees, with a radius of half a mile. Having found so much material of igneous origin at High Haume and Haverslack Hill, and all these extensive mines being so near, we have been very particular in our description as it will naturally form an element in considering the formation of our hematite ore. Besides the above, there are the mines of Schneider, Hannay, & Co at Old Hills, Whitriggs, and Marton, all within half a mile of the base of Haverslack hill, which, as stated before, is principally composed of *amygdaloid*. There are also mines at Carrkettle, of J. Rawlinson, and the splendid mines of Lindal Moor, Whinfield, Gillbrow, and Whitriggs Bottom, of Messrs Harrison, Ainslie, & Co; and at Lindal Cote, those of the Ulverston Mining Company; also at Dalton, those of J. Denny and Co, and J. Rawlinson; and near Highfield House, those of J. Clegg Esq. All these mining works are within a mile and a half of High Haume; besides, about a mile further, we have the Ulverston Mining Co's works at Stainton, Bolton Heads, Stone Close, and California; also Mr Wadham's at Crooklands; and Messrs Schneider, Hannay, and Co's at Newton. Perhaps we have omitted some, but we shall return to this subject.

Mining methods varied considerably across the Furness and Hodbarrow ore fields. In the narrow mineral veins around Urswick and Stainton, traditional methods of stoping were employed. In the veins, cross-veins, and ore-flats of Whitriggs - where the ore tended to mass in irregular pockets between the limestone bedding planes and natural rock fissures - the ore was systematically robbed, allowing the roof to collapse and reveal more ore. In the gigantic ore bodies (sops) of Park, Roanhead, Askam, Mouzell, Elliscales, and Lindal Moor, top slicing became widely adopted, a method similar to the board and pillar system of mining coal, the difference being that the pillars were also removed, allowing the roof to crush down on the sole while another "slice" was being worked underneath.

Top slicing required immense quantities of timber to support the working drifts, so in favourable conditions where the ore was harder the pillars were left unworked over a series of slices, creating large chambers with roofs supported by columns of hematite. The ore in the supporting pillars was exploited at a later date when the chambers had collapsed and subsidence crushed the ore to a friable mass.

The life expectancy of trial shafts under these conditions was short, and those sunk directly on the sops were quickly swallowed. The more permanent engine shafts tended to be situated on firmer ground but even these did not entirely escape the distortion caused by the ever encroaching subsidence.

The Hodbarrow deposit was, like the sops of Furness, large and irregular, though more akin to the flat deposits of the Egremont area in geological make-up. Top slicing was employed prior to 1922, but problems with subsidence and the close proximity of the sea brought about a change in policy and the adoption of bottom slicing. Ore was removed in slices from the sole of the deposit and the resultant voids filled with a slurry mixture of water and sand to prevent instability.

Water was a problem in the Furness mines. With the country rock being carboniferous limestone, underground "runners" and "feeders" were plentiful. On more than one occasion complete mines were washed out and the pumps overcome when subterranean watercourses were breached. Periods of sustained rainfall could flood certain pits within hours. The reports of the local mine inspectors give a fascinating insight into the extent of the problem, one of the most frequent comments being "the water's in".

Cornish beam engines were installed at Eure Pits (Dalton), Lindal Cote, Back Guards (Lindal), Whinfield (Lindal), Park, Roanhead, and Stank. Across the Duddon estuary there were Cornish engines at Hodbarrow, while Wicham Mine boasted two of the largest beam engines in the country at that particular time (1889-95). Horizontal pumping engines were common throughout the district, while during the early years of the 20th century several companies resorted to electrification as a means of improving their de-watering systems.

After the peak years of the 1870s and 1880s, decline was hastened by the gradual exhaustion of some of the older pits and the import of cheap iron ore from other countries, notably Spain. In Furness, the last big pit - Woodbine Pit, at North Stank - closed in 1946. The end came in 1960 when the Margaret Mine, an inclined drift in Henning Valley, Lindal, was bought out by a larger concern and subsequently closed.

Hodbarrow Mine continued in production till March 1968 when its greatly reduced workforce of a hundred-and-three men was laid off, bringing to an end hematite mining in the south of the county. Now, in the 1990s, just one working iron ore mine remains in Cumbria - the Florence Pit at Egremont.

Backbarrow Furnace was built in 1711 by local ironmasters to counter competition from a group of Cheshire businessmen, Edward Hall & Co, who, in the same year, erected a charcoal blast furnace at Cunsey on the shores of Windermere. The Backbarrow company was founded by John Machel, William Rawlinson, and Stephen Crossfield, to smelt hematite ore brought from the mines of the Furness peninsula. The initials of the proprietors are cast in the iron lintel of the furnace arch (this is a replacement lintel, the original being in Kendal's Abbot Hall Museum) as are the initials of the successors, Harrison, Ainslie & Co, Furness' longest running mining and smelting company. Backbarrow Furnace was modified many times before its closure during the 1960s. Despite its present ruinous state, Backbarrow is Cumbria's most complete charcoal blast furnace. *(photo, Dave Wheeler)*

Machinery of a bygone era lying rusting in the abandoned complex of Backbarrow ironworks. Above is the Lancashire boiler which powered the horizontal steam engine, below. The engine worked a bellows which provided the blast necessary for raising the furnace to the temperature suitable for converting hematite ore to pig iron. Originally, when the furnace was constructed in 1711, the bellows were powered by a waterwheel, situated in a wheel pit behind the present engine house. Backbarrow, along with Cunsey, is Cumbria's oldest charcoal blast furnace site. Others include Newland, Duddon, Penny Bridge, Nibthwaite, Lowwood, and Leighton. *(photos, Dave Wheeler)*

Duddon Furnace was erected in 1736 by the Cunsey company, of Cunsey ironworks near Windermere. Ore was shipped from Furness and off-loaded downstream of the smelting site, in the Duddon estuary. The furnace was taken over by Harrison, Ainslie & Co, of Newland Furnace, in 1828, and continued to produce pig iron till 1836. The blast furnaces of Cumbria were sited close to the coppice woodland, rather than the mining areas, to take advantage of the charcoal supplies. The site has been renovated in recent years, the furnace stack and associated buildings being reconstructed with authentic materials. To the right of the picture, the lintelled blowing arch looks out onto the bellows floor and waterwheel pit.

The casting floor is situated on the south side of the furnace stack. Beneath the almost perfect symmetry of the slate arch, molten iron once poured along a gutter in the earth floor to a series of moulds. The term "pig iron" is derived from this process, for the moulds had the appearance of piglets feeding off the mother sow.   *(photos, Anton & Sheila Thomas)*

In 1839 Henry William Schneider visited the Lake District and, while passing through Furness, realised the potential of the local hematite deposits. His partnership with Richard Hannay led to the establishment of the Barrow Hematite Steel Co, one of the North's largest and most successful iron mining and smelting firms. With mines at Whitriggs, Dalton, Park, and Stank, and a massive steel producing complex in the heart of Barrow itself, the company went from strength to strength, until the nationalisation of the steel industry wiped its name from the map.

The Primrose Pit, or Stank No.7, was situated on the county's most southerly hematite vein, in the village of Stank, midway between the towns of Dalton and Barrow. The picture, taken in 1879, shows the engine house under construction and the beam of a Cornish engine balancing on the bob wall. Note the Lancashire boiler and the large shaft-sinking kibble beneath the temporary headframe. *(photo, Dalton Castle Archive)*

The Stank iron mines of the Barrow Hematite Steel Co, 1879. In the centre of the picture is Stank No.1 Pit, complete with Cornish pumping engine and sheer-leg capstan (the tallest frame with sheave wheel), used for lowering replacement sections of pit-work, the great reciprocating rods which activated the pumps at the foot of the shaft. The two winding engines are situated in the building on the extreme right; again these are beam engines, but of the rotary variety, with winding crank fitted to the beam ends. To the immediate left of No.1 Pit is Stank No.2, a pumping shaft with balance bob connected to the pit-work to counter the weight and ease the load on the engine. On the brow of the hill is Stank No.5 Pit and, in the far distance, Yarlside No.11, near Furness Abbey. *(photo, Dalton Castle Archive)*

"Ga'an down't pit"... Stank miners, dressed in their "pinks", pose for a photo at the shaft top of No.1 Pit, 1879. Many miners came from Cornwall in search of work, and Stank Mine had more than its fair share of hard-rock men from the South-West. Note the candles stuck to the hats with balls of mud, the tea cans, the clay pipes, the duck-neb clogs and the bushy beards - traditionally worn to filter the air as a guard against silicosis, the hard-rock miners' curse. In the centre of the picture is one of the two pit cages, ready to descend with its complement of miners. The cages ran in guides, wooden rails seen here protruding from the shaft.   *(photo, Dalton Castle Archive)*

Over a century on - Stank No.1 Pit, the sole surviving Cornish engine house in the Furness peninsula. Most of the Stank engine houses were demolished after the mine closed in 1901. Explosives reduced these graceful monuments to heaps of masonry, ideal building materials for the shipyard managers' houses of Barrow's Abbey Road. The red sandstone blocks and grey limestone lintels and arches of Stank No.1 remain in the now peaceful countryside, protected against further damage by a preservation order. *(photo, Dave Wheeler)*

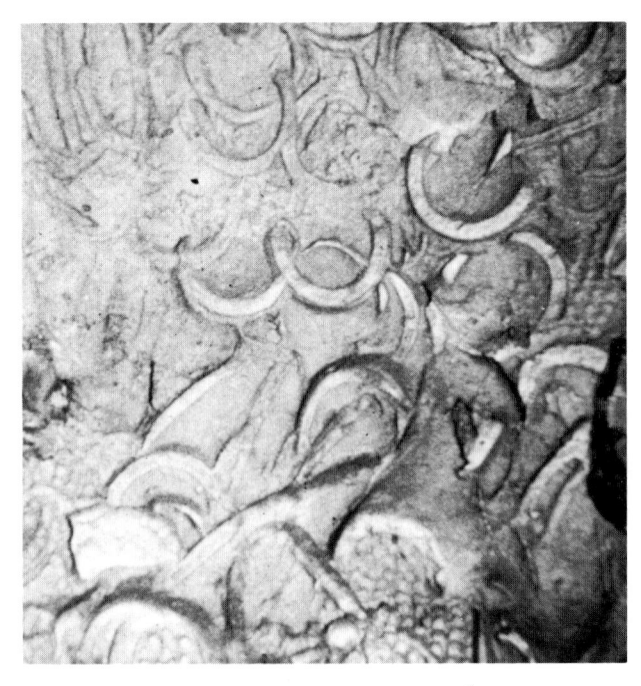

Clog prints in the mud floor of No.3 Level in No.8 Vein, Knockmurton Mine - a human link with the past and as fresh as if they had been made only yesterday.

An early ore wagon with rim wheels and detachable sides - handy for assembling in tight corners. This was discovered in the upper workings of No.1 and No.2 veins, Knockmurton Mine, Ennerdale. *(photos, Dave Bridge & Richard Hewer)*

A worked out ore flat in the Guttersby No.3 Pit, Bigrigg, near Whitehaven. Here the entire ore body has been removed and square pillars of deads and timber constructed to support the roof. The ore flats were sandwiched between the layers of the carboniferous limestone, the angle of dip corresponding to that of the country rock. *(photo, Anton & Sheila Thomas)*

For many years the B.30 Pit, one of Furness' most notorious pits, was Lindal Moor's main producer. Sunk during the 1850s, and known originally as Whitriggs Gin Pit (and more evocatively, the Old Peru), its three haulage levels gradually penetrated into the cross-veins of Henning Valley, the Waste workings at Marton, and the rich mineral ground of the Main Vein. Two thirds of the pit are now under water. This photograph was taken during a dry summer in the tramming level called Top Height, which, as the name implies, was the highest level of the B.30 workings. For most of the year the Top Height is totally submerged - only when the water level falls can access be gained through the workings of the B.45 Pit, at Marton, to the silent chambers of the Old Peru. The B.30 Pit closed on the 10th of October 1914. *(photo, Alen McFadzean)*

A roadway in the Waste workings beneath Lindal Moor. No tramlines were laid here - just planks placed on the mud for the miners to run their wheelbarrows along. This worked out section of the Lindal Moor Main Vein lies between the B.47 and B.41 pits, which were only eighty feet apart. Note the horizontal bedding of the carboniferous limestone and the deads stacked against the left hand wall and in the void on the right. *(photo, Alen McFadzean)*

Wood quickly rots away to a spongy mass in the damp conditions of the Furness iron mines. All that remains of a wooden wheelbarrow left in the Derby No.1 Pit workings in 1914 is the cast iron wheel.

The Derby No.1 Pit, situated in Moor Field, Marton, was worked by a steam winding engine installed on the old Rawlinson Shaft in 1906. Prior to this date ore was raised by horse gin and kibble. The kibbles were loaded at the face then transported by "whitechappels" (opposite) to the foot of the shaft, where they were hitched to the rope then hauled to grass. The Derby No.1 Pit was sunk in 1865 and closed for the last time in March 1914. *(photos, Alen McFadzean)*

A narrow stope or "ginnel" in the B.47 Pit ground on Lindal Moor. The Main Vein was, for the most part, a broad mass of hematite interspersed with webs of barren rock - but in some areas it degenerated into a series of parallel veins divided by walls of limestone. Ore from this section was raised initially by horse gin at the B.47, though as the 19th century progressed and the Lindal Moor mines became interlinked, it was trammed to the B.30 Pit in Henning Valley and raised by steam winder.
(photo, Alen McFadzean)

The Derby Rise, the 25 ft connection between the workings of the B.30 Pit and the Derby No.1 Pit. These pits were situated in different mineral royalties and worked by different companies. The "B" pits were leased from the Duke of Buccleuch and worked by Harrison, Ainslie & Co, while the Derby pits were leased from the Earl of Derby and worked by a succession of companies, the most recent being the Millom & Askam Hematite Iron Co. The Rise was a B.30 trial which, being on the mineral boundary, broke into the neighbouring pit.   *(photo, Alen McFadzean)*

Tribute workings in the 68 yard Level of the Derby No.1 Pit, Marton. Tributers were rewarded by the ton so paid little regard to the efficient running of the pit - they took the easiest ore by the easiest methods, a situation which had the effect of turning pits into complicated honeycombs of workings which became nightmares to control. Ore was robbed away and the resultant voids allowed to collapse - as is the case here. The roof of the chamber has dropped in and crushed the timbers of the haulage level. The Derby No.1, though, was considered a structurally stable pit on the one hand - but a honeycomb of the worst variety on the other. *(photo, Alen McFadzean)*

Looking along the Top Height of the B.30 Pit towards the deep water and the silent darkness of the Lindal Moor Mines. Nearly eighty years have passed since the men of Marton and Lindal pushed their heavy tubs along these rocky tunnels. Horses were never used underground in the Furness iron mines. The owners preferred to rely on the brute strength of the indigenous population and immigrants from Cornwall, Ireland, Wales, and the iron producing counties of middle England. Iron mining was extremely labour intensive - but this can be blamed as much on the geology as on local tradition. *(photo, Alen McFadzean)*

WOLFRAM

by David Blundell

Wolfram mining in Cumbria was confined to one site, Carrock Mine, situated in Grainsgill - a tributary of the river Caldew - four-and-a-half miles south of Caldbeck and twelve miles west of Penrith. Carrock was the only locality outside the counties of Cornwall and Devon to have produced wolfram. Along with Castle-an-Dinas Mine, near St Austell in Cornwall (worked 1915 to 1958), it was the only mine in the country where wolfram was the sole ore produced.

The mine has worked spasmodically since 1854, but never for very long as mining is only viable when the price of tungsten is at its peak. The last period of working finished in October 1981.

Wolfram was previously produced in Britain as a by-product of the tin mines of Devon and Cornwall and was, prior to 1898, regarded by miners as a nuisance in ore dressing, due to the difficulties of separating it from the cassiterite (tin ore). After this date, demand rose for wolfram for use in the production of tungsten high-speed steel and tungsten cutting tools. In Cornwall, the mines of the Cambourne-Redruth area dominated the production of wolfram, with the mines of East Pool and Agar, South Crofty, Carn Brea, and Tincroft being the major producers. Carrock Mine, even in its heyday, was never a major producer of wolfram. For example, in 1916 Carrock produced twenty tons of WO_3 concentrate, slightly under 5.5% of the total national production for that year. With the closure of most of the Cornish mines, British production of tungsten ores in world terms is now insignificant. Wolfram is now imported from the USA, Australia, Canada, Bolivia, Portugal, and the Republic of Korea.

The ores produced at Carrock Mine were galena (PbS), wolfram ($Fe_1Mn_1WO_3$), and scheelite ($CaWO_4$), the last two named being the chief ores of tungsten. Traditionally this metal was almost exclusively used for making the filaments in light bulbs, vacuum and x-ray tubes. With the growing use of nuclear reactors for generating electricity, tungsten has become important as a cladding for fuel rods containing uranium and plutonium oxides because it is non-reactive, has a high melting point, and is a good conductor of heat. It is widely used in cemented carbides, tool steels, and tungsten metal mill products.

The geology of the Carrock area consists of several mineralised veins dipping west at about 80° and tending northwards across the lower part of Grainsgill Beck, where they have been worked from Carrock Mine. The veins traverse the northernmost outcrop of the Skiddaw granite (which is mostly converted to gneiss) and the adjacent hornfels and gabbro rocks of the north. The upper parts of the granite in the gneissenised zones are above Grainsgill and take the form of a dome which attains its maximum elevation between the eastern spur of Coombe Height, and the Caldew and Grainsgill valleys. The roof contact falls fairly steeply in all directions to pass beneath the metamorphosed Skiddaw slates. The three principal veins, going from west to east, are the Smith Vein, the Harding Vein, and the Emerson Vein.

The mine is situated in the steep-sided valley of the Grainsgill Beck, with the main adit at a height of 1,115 ft AOD. The veins cross the beck at approximately 90°, rendering the mine easily worked by a series of adit levels driven north and south into the valley sides. No workings have been developed below the main adit, and as the adit is above the valley bottom, it was not necessary to resort to pumping or winding to work the mine. Ore from upper workings was scraped and tipped down a series of internal ore-passes into hoppers on the main adit level then run into tubs and hauled out of the mine to the mill. The country rock is competent and the majority of the stopes and levels are self-supporting. Only small quantities of timber were required, where the levels pass through the overlying boulder clay.

Up to 1913 all rock drilling was done by hand, but following the take-over of the mine by the Carrock Mining Syndicate, an air-compressor, driven by a gas engine, was installed to power three rock drills. In the last phase of working, a number of Joy Sullivan double drum compressed-air winches were in use in the mine, to scrape ore along higher sub-levels to ore-passes, replacing the method previously used of hand-loading wheelbarrows and tipping the ore down the passes. In development drives in the mine, Eimco compressed-air loading shovels were used to load rock and ore into mine tubs. The method of operation is to run the loader forward on its rails, into a pile of rock left after blasting, with the shovel lowered. With a mine tub coupled to the rear of the loader, the bucket on the loading shovel swings rapidly from the horizontal to the vertical, throwing the material back into the tub. This minimises the amount of backbreaking labour involved in loading rock and ore into tubs.

The principal workings have been on the Harding Vein, which varies in width from a few inches in the granite to over five feet in the gabbro. It consists mainly of quartz with distributions of wolfram and scheelite, together with a range of other minerals. This vein has been proved to a length of over 1,500 feet, on both sides of the Grainsgill valley, by surface and underground work.

A little exploration was carried out on the Smith Vein in the early part of the century from the surface where it was found to contain arsenopyrite and scheelite. Later, the 1942-43 exploration crosscut to the Harding Vein was extended westwards to the Smith Vein. It was explored to the north and south with not very satisfactory results but was subsequently worked during the latest phase of operations, giving a vein width of approximately two feet. The Smith Vein has not been worked to the south of Grainsgill Beck.

The Emerson Vein has a long history of spasmodic working on five levels on the northern slope of the valley, and one trial level on the Coombe Height (south) side. All the adits have now caved in, and the levels are for the most part inaccessible. The wolfram content of this vein is said to have been rich in places, but had a very patchy distribution. In early 1980, a crosscut was driven east from the adit level of the mine to the Emerson Vein, and some driving was completed to the north for about 700 feet, but with very little production. This part of the mine has poor natural ventilation.

The earliest recorded working in the area took place in 1852, by F W Emerson of Penzance, Cornwall, who was intending to mine for copper and lead ores on the east-west veins which are about 200 yards long, and run between the Harding and Emerson Veins halfway up Brandy Gill. A mining lease for lead was not granted by the owner of the mineral rights, and so Emerson turned his attention to the most easterly of the veins, which now bears his name. Work was also carried out on a small trial in Brandy Gill. All work had ceased by 1858.

In 1863, Leicester M Hutchinson & Co, and later from 1875-77, M Hutchinson & Co, worked the lead veins in Brandy Gill. Two levels were driven in the west bank of the gill and joined by a rise. It is reported that there was a promising show of galena at first, but it was later found that the ore-body was very small. Production in 1872 was four tons of galena, giving three tons of lead, and in 1874, five-and-a-half tons of galena giving four tons of lead and twenty-nine ounces of silver. In 1872-73, small scale workings took place on the Harding Vein on the south side of Grainsgill valley, at the outcrop of the vein. Wolfram was produced by hand-sorting but no production records exist.

In 1902, Carrock Mines Ltd, under James Harding, of Penrith, took a take-note for the mine and commenced prospecting works, mainly on the vein subsequently named after him and also at three levels on the Emerson Vein. By 1905 the mine had closed, having produced thirty-seven tons of wolfram ore.

The mine did not stand idle for long, for in 1906 two Germans, William Boss and Frederick Boehm, re-financed the operations, and under the name of the Cumbrian Mining Co Ltd the mill was extended, and for a time both day and night shifts operated at the mine and the mill. The workforce reached a peak of a hundred-and-five, evenly split between the surface and underground workers. Production averaged twenty-three tons per annum, valued at £60 per ton for most of the period, but reaching £118 per ton in 1907, when sixty-four tons were produced. Four tons of arsenic were produced in 1911, valued at £5 per ton. By the end of 1911 production had ceased, and the following year the company was in liquidation, with only the caretaker, William Wilson of Caldbeck, remaining on the payroll.

1913 saw the formation of the Carrock Mining Syndicate, a group of steel manufacturers under the management of Captain Anthony Wilson, of Thornthwaite Grange, near Keswick, who also managed the Thornthwaite and Threlkeld mines. The work was partly government financed, the mill being reconstructed and equipped with hand-picking belts, crushing rolls, jigs, screens, Deister sand tables, Wilfey tables, and Vanners. The concentrates were roasted in a half-ton capacity hand-raked furnace, to remove the arsenic, which was collected from the flues. Power was supplied by generators driven by pelton wheels, assisted during times of water shortage by a gas engine. The remains of this operation can still be seen by the side of the beck adjacent to the Harding Vein (south). Stoping was carried out in the Penny Level (Harding Vein south), Harding Level on the vein (north), along with some work on the Emerson Vein. Almost 14,000 tons of ore were mined, and 10,116 tons milled, which produced almost 100 tons of 16% WO_3 concentrate.

With the close of the First World War, government support was withdrawn, while at the same time the market was swamped with stocks of tungsten concentrates as governments off-loaded their strategic stockpiles. This caused the complete collapse of the market for tungsten concentrates and they became virtually impossible to sell. The previous year the same concentrate would have fetched £178 per ton. By late 1918 the workforce had dropped from around a hundred, to twenty-five at the time of closure of the underground workings. In 1919 a few workers were involved in washing zinc blende prior to the mill being dismantled later that year.

The site remained silent until the fall of Burma in 1942. Burma was at that time an important source of tungsten. Faced with a possible shortage, the country again turned to Carrock. The Ministry of Supply, in conjunction with Non-Ferrous Minerals Development Ltd, attempted to prove the existence of 80,000 to 100,000 tons of tungsten ore. The exploratory work commenced in June 1942 and continued till October 1943. The services of a Canadian Royal Engineers tunnelling company was used, as no local skilled labour was available. The thirty-five Canadians were billeted in barracks built on the mine. At the end of 1942, twenty-five Canadians left for other duties and their place was taken by Spanish Pioneers and Italian POWs. A new crosscut level was driven to the Harding Vein

(No.2 or Canadian Level, the present entrance to the mine), some sixty feet below the old Harding (No.1) Level. The crosscut was extended to the Smith Vein, as well as driving north and south on the Harding Vein, totalling two-thousand feet and at a cost of £5 per foot, with a further £5,000 spent on compressors, pipelines, buildings and roads. It was proposed to erect a small mill (suitable for incorporation into a larger set-up later) but this was never built. Sampling was carried out on the Harding Vein (north and south), Smith and Emerson Veins, proving the existence of 51,000 tons of wolfram in excess of 1.09% mineral. No stoping was carried out and the Ministry of Supply closed the project down in October 1943, having declined to carry out a programme of diamond drilling, recommended by their consultants, Messrs James Jackson and J D Wilson, who claimed that the target had been reached. By this time the tungsten supply position had improved.

The next period of interest in the mine was in 1951-52 with the outbreak of the Korean War (Korea being an important producer of wolfram) and a rise in the price of tungsten metal. Durham Chemicals took an interest in the mine, but encountered stiff opposition for any development from the National Trust and various local bodies, due to the mine's situation in the then proposed Lake District National Park. Before the problem could be resolved the price of tungsten fell again and Durham Chemicals withdrew without carrying out any work on site.

In 1971 World Wide Energy (U.K.) Ltd, a wholly-owned subsidiary of WECO Development Corporation of Denver, Colorado, USA, leased the mine and 3,500 acres surrounding it. Their assessment of the ore deposits was based wholly on the results of the exploration of 1942-43, with only limited sampling taking place for confirmation. A mill was constructed and some underground development took place on the old Harding Level. The mill ran for only a few weeks in 1972, on 230 tons of wolfram ore with a grade of 1.55%, before the company decided to withdraw. They put the mill on standby in July 1972, after spending £250,000. The price of wolfram had fallen from £38 per ton in 1970 to only £16 in 1972.

The shutdown lasted until 1976 when WECO granted a one-year lease to Carrock Fell Mining Ltd (a subsidiary of Amalgamated Industrials Ltd) with an option to enter into a joint venture agreement at the end of the lease period in August 1977. Robertson Research International Ltd, of North Wales, were appointed as technical consultants in September 1976. The mine and mill came into production in April 1977, with the aim of processing 12,500 tonnes per annum, or 60 tonnes per eight-hour day. The operation became profitable during the first six months of 1978 and employed sixteen men underground, with a further eight in the mill. At the end of the option period the joint venture was taken up. Twelve months later Carrock Fell Mining was purchased by the National Carbonising Co (Energy) Ltd, who continued the joint venture on the same basis as the previous company - 62.14% shares, with World Wide Energy (U.K.) Ltd at 37.86%. Production of ore was running at 16,000 tonnes per annum, giving 200 tonnes of 65% wolfram concentrates. Ore was produced from the Harding Vein (north and South), Wilson Vein, Waterfall Vein, and from the Emerson Vein via a crosscut driven from the Canadian Level in 1979-80.

The workforce totalled thirty when the mine closed in October 1981. The price of wolfram concentrates had again fallen, coupled with the company's difficulty in disposing of the fine tailings from the mill, due to the restrictive regulations on the size of the lagoons imposed by the National Park authorities. They had to resort to pumping them as a slurry into the old stopes on the Harding Vein (south). Problems were encountered regarding the high levels of arsenic found in the coarse tailings from the mill, which made them unsuitable for use an an aggregate, because of the risk of poisonous dust being released into the atmosphere.

The mine was put into mothballs on a care and maintenance basis. A new company purchased the lease in November 1982, part of the Minworth group of companies, based in Derbyshire. No further work was carried out, and in the spring of 1986 mining and milling equipment was removed from site, trackwork lifted, and smaller buildings removed.

It is notable that in the past the threat, or actuality, of war has brought Carrock Mine into production. It is to be hoped that this course of events will not be responsible for the mine's future working.

The strike of the main veins, Smith, Harding, and Emerson, can be clearly identified on site, to the north and south of Grainsgill Beck. Following the abandonment of the lease in 1988, the 1971 mill and associated buildings were cleared completely and the site, along with the tailings lagoon, was bulldozed and graded back to a close approximation of the original contours. The adit portals were destroyed and sealed, although mine drainage water still finds its way to day through the collapse at the Canadian Level, the main adit to the mine. Open stopes on the Harding Vein (north) were sealed with rails concreted over the stopes. The only remains of buildings left on the site are those on the south side of Grainsgill Beck, the concrete bases of hoppers constructed in 1913 by the Carrock Mining Syndicate.

1913 saw the formation of the Carrock Mining Syndicate, a group of steel manufacturers under the management of Captain Anthony Wilson, of Thornthwaite Grange, near Keswick. The work was partly government financed, the mill being reconstructed and equipped with hand-picking belts, crushing rolls, jigs, screens, Deister sand tables, Wilfey tables, and Vanners. The concentrates were roasted in a half-ton capacity hand-raked furnace, to remove the arsenic, which was collected from the flues. Power was supplied by generators driven by pelton wheels, assisted during times of water shortage by a gas engine.

The remains of this operation can still be seen by the side of the beck adjacent to the Harding Vein. Today they are the only tangible surface remains of Cumbria's wolfram mining industry. *(photo, Dave Blundell)*

Overtaken by time, a redundant jaw crusher stands among the spoil beneath the Carrock mill. *(photo, Dave Blundell)*

Carrock Mine as it was in March 1985. In the foreground stands the ore-bin, from which a conveyer leads to the secondary crusher and mill buildings.

Following the abandonment of the lease in 1988, the 1971 mill and associated buildings were cleared completely and the site, along with the tailings lagoon, was bulldozed and graded back to a close approximation of the original contours. *(photo, Dave Blundell)*

Work commenced in June 1942 on a new level and continued till October 1943. The services of a Canadian Royal Engineers tunnelling company was used, as no local skilled labour was available. The crosscut was driven to the Harding Vein (No.2 or Canadian Level, the present entrance to the mine), some sixty feet below the old Harding (No.1) Level. The crosscut was extended to the Smith Vein, as well as driving north and south on the Harding Vein, totalling two-thousand feet and at a cost of £5 per foot.
(photo, Dave Blundell)

Underground in Carrock Mine. An air-receiver and pipework abandoned to the darkness.

A distinctive rib of white quartz in the roof of a working horizon deep in Carrock.
(photos, Ronnie Calvin)

LEAD & ZINC

by Ian Matheson and Chris Jones

Lead occurs widely. It is a soft metal, is easy to work and to smelt, and can be reduced from its ore in an ordinary camp fire. It was one of the first metals to be discovered, having been in use for at least 8000 years. The earliest known example is a necklace of lead beads found at Catal Huyuk in Anatolia. Much later it was used by the Romans to make water pipes, cisterns, and for roofing. When the Romans left Britain civilisation declined, and so too did the need for minerals and mining skills. Throughout medieval times only relatively small amounts of lead were used for roofing churches and other buildings, and it was not until the 16th century that a boom in the building of great houses brought about an increased demand in lead for roofs and guttering. In the 18th and 19th centuries Britain was the world's largest producer, and many new uses were found for the metal. It was used in lead based paints, lead crystal glass, and to make bullets and lead shot. In the 20th century demand increased further as lead was used for electrical cables, batteries, and as an additive in petrol, but in Britain lead mining declined as cheaper lead was imported from Spain, Australia, and the USA. The last British lead mines finally closed in the 1960s.

The most important ore of lead is the sulphide, known as galena, which contains about 86% lead, and is a brittle, heavy, silver-grey mineral which forms cubic crystals. It is usually found in fissures resulting from faults and joints in limestone, and in veins and pockets in volcanic rocks. It occurs in strings of quartz, fluorspar, calcite, or barytes and is often associated with zinc and copper, and usually contains a small proportion of silver, which can add to its value. The gangue materials form much the greater part of the content of a vein and used to be regarded as waste. Now they are often the more important product, and the metal ores are regarded as a by-product.

Zinc is often found in association with lead. The most common ore is sphalerite, known as blende, or black jack. It is used to make dry cell batteries, in paints, and for galvanising iron to prevent rusting. In the early days it was a waste material, and being of a similar density to galena there was difficulty in separating the ores.

The simplest method of concentrating ores was by gravity. The ore was first crushed to a powder by bucking with hammers, or by using stamps or crushing rollers, and then processed in water. Jigging was the method by which the fine ore was agitated in tanks of water so that the heavier particles settled to the bottom and the lighter rock particles were left on the top and could be skimmed off. Buddling involved washing ore in a fine stream of water, when the lighter particles were carried further, and so separated from the heavier metal. These techniques were not effective in separating galena, sphalerite and barytes, which have similar densities, and it was not until 1898 that the Elmore flotation process made this possible. This used the affinity of sulphides for certain oils, which could then be floated off in water. Later, gas bubbles were used to enhance this process.

In the Lake District zinc was produced mainly at the mines of Force Crag, Threlkeld and Thornthwaite. Lead was found in many places but the principal mining fields were in the Helvellyn, Newlands, and Caldbeck areas.

There are no records or remains of very early mining in the Lake District, and whilst it is probable that the metal was extracted from pre-Roman times, any traces which might have been left have long since been obliterated by later workings. As new mining and smelting techniques have been developed it has often been thought worthwhile to reopen on a much larger scale old workings which had been abandoned as no longer viable, and to reprocess old waste heaps. This reworking of old mining fields results in the destruction of the older remains and wipes the record clean. Most of the remains which are now visible date from the 19th and 20th centuries.

There are few records for the centuries after the Romans left, and although there are references in medieval documents pertaining to land grants and so forth, which relate to lead mining, there are few detailed records dating from earlier than the 16th century. At that time the Crown took an interest in mineral resources, and in 1564 the Company of Mines Royal was formed. There were twenty-four shares, eleven of which were initially owned by the Augsburg firm of Haug, Langnaur & Co, and royalties were payable to Queen Elizabeth I. Their principal interest was in copper, which was mined at Keswick and at Coniston, and experienced miners, known as "Dutchmen", were imported from Germany to carry out the work. Lead was required for separating the silver from copper ore, but apparently none was available locally, for at first this was imported from Alston Moor, indicating that there were no local lead mines producing at that time. The Elizabethans eventually operated lead mines in the Derwent area at Stoneycroft, Brandlehow, Barrow and Thornthwaite, and in the Caldbeck Fells at Red Gill and Roughtongill. In 1564 a lead mine was opened in Greenhead Gill at Grasmere, but this venture was not successful and the mine closed in 1573. It was never reopened and the remains, which can still be seen, are remarkable as they are truly Elizabethan. At the same time Goldscope Mine, in German "Gottes Gab", meaning Gods Gift, was successfully worked for copper, but it was not until much later, in 1852, that lead was discovered there and became the principal ore to be extracted at that mine.

The Company of Mines Royal was not profitable, for between 1564 and 1600 metals to the value of £68,103 had been sold but £104,709 had been expended. The Civil War contributed to an unfavourable economic climate, and it is said that in 1661 Cromwell's troops destroyed the smelter at Brigham, near Keswick, and enlisted some of the miners. Mining in the Lake District was therefore in decline during much of the 17th century, and it was not until the end of that century that mining resumed on any substantial scale. It would appear that another party of "Dutchmen" came to the district in 1690, and lead was mined at Hartsop, near Brotherswater, on the side of Barrow, near Derwentwater, and nearby in Stoneycroft Gill, where a smelter was also constructed. An early mining disaster took place here, for in order to sink a shaft in the bed of the gill the stream had been diverted and a dam built. Without warning the dam burst, and the water cascading down the gill flooded the shaft, drowning the men below and burying them in sand. It is said that their bodies were never recovered.

Water was always a problem for miners, but never more so than in the early days. It had to be lifted from the workings by bucket or by hand pump. Work often had to cease during winter months. A letter written by mining engineer David Davies, about 1690, relating to Barrow Mine, contained several references to the water being too strong. A level was driven under the sole of the work to clear the water, 300 fathoms in length and wrought night and day for seven years. When they came to clear the water they found that "the ore did not continue two fathoms deeper"! Lead mining was also carried on at Greenside during this period, and may have been started as early as 1650 near the summit of the mountain, where the ore outcropped at the surface. Dressed ore was taken by packhorse over Sticks Pass to the smelter at Stoneycroft, a distance of ten miles up hill and down dale.

Progress in mining is intermittent, for success depends on many factors. Luck, demand, a suitable economic climate, the availability of capital, and improvements in technology all play their part, so few mines have been worked continuously for long periods. During the 18th century iron mining flourished, and there was some mining of copper for a time, but there is no record of great or continuous activity in the Lake District so far as lead mining was concerned. The mines at Barrow were worked by various people, and Thornthwaite Mine was worked in the 18th century. Smelters were operated at Roughtongill and at Hartsop, but lead extraction in the North-West in the 18th century was largely the work of the London Lead Company at Alston Moor. Some lead mines in Patterdale were worked about 1750, but it is not known for how long. Top Level at Greenside was driven in 1690 some forty fathoms below the summit, and stoped out to the surface, but the mine had been abandoned for several years when plans were being made soon after the turn of the 18th century to re-establish them, leading, in 1822, to the formation of the Greenside Mining Company. This mine was to become the richest in the area, and was to be worked more or less continuously for the next one-hundred-and-fifty years, though not without some setbacks and changes of ownership.

Some 2,400,000 tons of lead ore were produced during the life of the mine, and 2,000,000 ounces of silver. In the early days the dressed ore was taken elsewhere to be smelted, firstly to Stoneycroft Gill, and then, from 1820, to Alston where the London Lead Company had erected an up to date smelter. During the 1830s a smelter was built at the foot of Lucy Tongue Gill, and a flue arched with stone was cut out of the bed rock, ending a mile away on the Stang, where there was a stack. The course of this flue can easily be traced today, and part of the stack is still standing. This smelter was in operation until the beginning of the 20th century, when it was decided to close it, and to send the dressed ore by train from Troutbeck to Newcastle-on-Tyne for processing.

By 1850 the upper part of the mine was worked out, and the Willie Shaft was begun from Low Horse Level. At the same time the Lucy Tongue Adit was started. Its entrance was located just above the smelt mill, 82 fathoms below Low Horse Level. Working in three shifts, twenty-four hours a day, this took sixteen years to complete, and followed a circuitous course to take advantage of a soft vein. Even with two men per shift hand boring they were not able to cut more than 120 yards per year.

Greenside Mine was one of the most valuable in the north of England, but it is unique because it was the first mine in Britain to use electrical winding and underground haulage, generating its own electricity by means of water turbines. Formerly, power was provided by two turbines and several waterwheels, and by two underground hydraulic engines. The old upper levels of the mine were bricked up and used to store water for these turbines. The Victorian pipework and the breached internal dams are still in place, as are seven-hundred feet of miners ladders descending from Glencoyne Level almost to Lucy Tongue, which were subsequently put in to provide an alternative escape route from the mine.

In 1890 William Borlase became manager, and he persuaded the company to modernise and to install a hydro-electric plant. Water was brought from dams built at Red Tarn and Keppel Cove Tarn, two miles distant from the mine, and conveyed in a partly-covered flume which follows the contour at the foot of Catstye Cam for well over a mile. This discharged into a 15 inch pipe giving a fall of 420 feet to a "Y" piece which directed the water through a vortex turbine and a pelton wheel powering two 100 hp dynamos. The electricity was taken into the mine via the Lucy Tongue Level. The vortex turbine and generator provided the power for a 50 hp winding motor at the head of Smiths Shaft, situated underground two miles away from the generating station, and for a 14 hp electric locomotive working in the Lucy Tongue and hauling out to day over a distance of one-and-a-half miles. The pelton wheel provided electrical power for a 50 hp motor driving a compressor and for two 10 hp motors driving pumps on the 60 and 90 fathom levels. All the lighting, both underground and in the mill and office buildings, was supplied from the main generating station. The capacity of this plant was increased over the years as demand grew, and it operated until 1936 when the National Grid was brought in. There are extensive remains still to be seen of the system of dams and leats which gathered every available drop of water from the mountain sides.

Twice there were serious floods caused by the breaching of the dams. The first was in 1870 when a great storm partially burst the Top Dam up towards Sticks Pass. Water flooding down Lucy Tongue Gill carried away part of the silver refining building, and it is said that a 1000 ounce plate of silver went with it and was never recovered. The second was when the earth dam in Keppel Cove was breached. High on the slopes of Helvellyn the tarn, which remains dry to this day, once covered an area of six acres, and was contained by an earth dam forty feet high and a hundred feet thick at its base. During the night of 29th October 1927 a hole fifty feet wide was torn in the dam, and the tarn emptied itself down the valley towards Glenridding, two-and-a-half miles away. Much damage was done, but amazingly there was no loss of life. This disaster nearly closed the mine, as the company paid heavy compensation, but new capital was found and the mine continued to work until 1934 when the low price of lead stopped operations. In 1936 it was taken over by the Basinghall Mining Syndicate who carried out much redevelopment, and the mine became profitable once more. By the end of the war however the workings had bottomed out into the Skiddaw slate, and it was apparent that the ore reserves were becoming exhausted. Despite a programme of exploration started in 1947 to find new deposits, no ore was found, and the mine moved towards its final closure which took place in 1962.

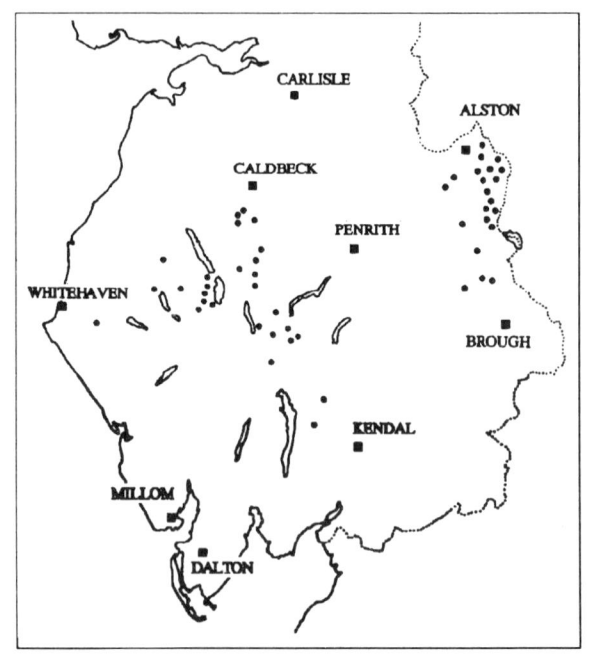

The general disposition of lead and zinc mines in Cumbria

Both before and since the closure there have been attempts at landscaping, and most of the buildings have been demolished or converted into bothies and a Youth Hostel. Much of the land has been acquired by the National Park and the National Trust. The bare bones of the mine remain, and there are miles of old leats contouring the fellside from the dams at Red Tarn, Brown Cove, Keppel Cove, High Dam and Glencoyne. The Lucy Tongue was blown in, but water still drains from the rubble; the smelter flue traverses the hillside, and there is much of interest to be seen in and above Lucy Tongue Gill. It is still possible to reach the Lucy Tongue Level via the Glencoyne Adit, which has been gated by the Cumbria Amenity Trust Mining History Society, but this involves a 700 foot descent down the old ladderway, requiring great care.

Elsewhere in the Lake District there is not much remaining of the lead mines at Thornthwaite and Barrow, nor of those in the Caldbeck Fells. There are workings at Hartsop and at Eagle Crag which are worth examining, whilst at Wythburn Mine as well as underground workings the old self-acting incline and drum house can still be seen. Goldscope, in the Newlands Valley, was mined for copper by the Elizabethans, but in 1852 the copper adit reached the lead vein, and some 5000 tons of ore were raised over the next twelve years. The lead vein is no longer accessible however, and the interesting remains at Goldscope are those of the Elizabethan copper workings, which have been modified in some places by the 19th century miners.

The last mine to work in the Lake District National Park was Force Crag, which has had a long and varied history. It is thought that there may have been some activity in Elizabethan times, but there was no work of any great consequence until the early years of the 19th century. Several leases were taken out, but it was not until 1840 that any quantity of ore was produced, and between then and 1865, 590 tons of lead and 1300 ounces of silver were sold, the ore being carted to Maryport and then shipped on to Liverpool. The coming of the Keswick and Penrith Railway, reaching Braithwaite in 1865, would have simplified this operation, but falling lead prices caused the mine to become unprofitable and it closed in that year. Two years later another company was formed to reopen the mine, this time to extract barytes, and after renovating the mine, which had become derelict after two years of closure, they were quickly into production. Transportation became much more organised, and ore was brought down from High Force by slushing it down wooden flumes to the mill, using water as a lubricant, and an inclined tramway two miles in length was built to Braithwaite. However, once again the mine became unprofitable due to unstable prices, and the banks foreclosed in 1879. 5,300 tons of barytes had been produced.

The mine was not reopened until about 1907, and this time zinc was the main product. Fifty men were employed, and a new mill was constructed, but in 1911 the mine closed again due to bankruptcy. A new company opened the following year and carried out modifications to the mill, installing an Elmore flotation plant to separate the ore, one of the first to be used in Britain. They also spent a lot of money driving a new level, Zero Level, but the returns could not support all this heavy investment and yet again the mine closed. When the Great War created new demands, and a subsidy was payable on zinc, the mine was reopened, and the mill brought up to date with the latest technology. After the war the subsidy was removed, and it closed again in 1922. This pattern of intermittent working was to continue over the years due to the varied demand for minerals and to the uncertainties of mining.

During the 1930s barytes was mined from High Force, which had not been worked since 1880. A track was driven up the fellside so that equipment and ore could be transported by lorry, and on the outbreak of the Second World War the mine was acquired by Tampimex Oil Products Ltd, who widened the track and built a new mill to produce barytes, which was used in the manufacture of explosives. It is this mill which can be seen at the present time. The track proved unsatisfactory and an aerial ropeway was constructed from High Force to the mill, 740 feet below, traces of which still exist. During the winter of 1947 the mine was totally cut off by snow for six weeks, and when access was regained it was found to be completely flooded. As pumping equipment was not available it was decided to close the mine, having raised some 35,000 tons of barytes. Two years later the La Porte Chemical Co took over, and having established that there were reserves of 100,000 tons of barytes, decided to drive an incline to a height of 325 feet above No.3 Level, and then to put up a rise to drain the flooded High Force workings from below. The incline was driven for 1100 feet without finding the vein, and a 40 foot rise had been put in a short distance from the top when the company had a change of policy and pulled out.

The mine was disused for eight years until, in 1960, McKechnie Brothers of Widnes restarted the operation and soon broke through into the workings above, which had been flooded since 1947. They too mined barytes, much of which was taken down the La Porte Incline using heavy scrapers dragged by winches and assisted by water. Some of this machinery is still in place. The company carried out an evaluation of reserves in No.1 Level, and estimated 40,000 tons at 10% zinc, but this was not developed and McKechnies closed the mine in 1966 when the known barytes reserves in the High Force area were mined out.

Over the next fifteen years three more companies attempted to work the lower part of the mine for lead and zinc, but none was successful. What may well prove to be the final attempt commenced in 1984, when the New Coledale Mining Co was formed to extract zinc, lead, and barytes from the low levels on a part time basis. The first task was to get the mill into working order and to restore the entrances to No.1 and Zero levels. At first the company concentrated on barytes, but later shifted to zinc. This operation ended in 1990 when a massive collapse occurred in Zero Level, long known as the "unsuccessful level". Water backed up to No.1 Level, so it was necessary to rescue equipment ahead of the rising water. The scale of the collapse was such that to clear it was beyond the resources of the company, and all work was stopped. The mine was on a short lease, and the landowners, the National Trust, are not in favour of a working mine in the Lake District fells, so it seems unlikely that mining will ever again take place at Force Crag. As a consequence of the more or less continuous history of mining, from the mid 19th century to the present time, the mine is much better preserved than most, and so it is unique. It is to be hoped that it will not be destroyed and landscaped like the mines of Greenside and Carrock, but will be preserved as part of our heritage.

Alston and the North Pennines

The area with which we will now concern ourselves is the highest and most northerly part of the Pennine chain situated in the county of Cumbria, an area which is without doubt one of the most inhospitable in the whole of England. Yet it is an area which has hidden some of England's greatest mineral wealth, a wealth which is still being exploited in some small way to this day.

The mining of lead and its associated ores is an ancient industry which can trace its roots back to Roman times and possibly beyond. The Romans operated lead mines throughout their huge empire, especially in Spain, so it would seem certain that they would know of the North Pennine's wealth and exploit it, given that they were so close at the nearby great wall of Hadrian.

After the Romans, little is known of the fate of this area although the use of Anglo-Danish terminology in local mining dialect suggests that the mineral wealth of the area was appreciated.

After the Norman conquest, evidence of mining activity is non-existent until we have the first recorded note in 1130 for rent on a silver mine on Alston Moor (silver was often extracted from lead ore) which was a hundred shillings, an astronomical sum. From that time there are sporadic reports of other silver mines in the area, perhaps supplying the mint known to be operating in Carlisle. It was around this time that whole new markets for lead were opening up with a massive increase in the construction of religious houses and castles for the new aristocracy. Indeed, lead was not only roofing English buildings, it is known that a hundred cartloads were dispatched to Clairvaux in France. One can do little but wonder at a journey which would have taken the lead from the rugged moorland of Alston by packhorse to the Tyne. From there it would have been shipped to Rotterdam before going on to Clairvaux.

In the 13th century the mines changed hands several times under the ownership of the kings of Scotland, but of mining in the 14th century little is known. The 15th century saw a considerable growth of activity and by 1468 the English king, Edward IV, had made agreements enabling him to receive a twelfth part of all the precious metals found. Throughout the rest of the century the kings of England had active interests in the area, especially in the mine of Fletcheras, between the South Tyne and the Nent valleys, where there is still evidence of ancient workings.

These primitive workings continued under royal patronage until the 16th century when Henry VIII appointed a German, Joachim Hoegstre, to be his master of mines. Hoegstre was the father of Daniel Höchstetter who appears later in the development of the copper industry at Keswick and Coniston. From Hoegstre's work sprang a far more professional approach to the development of metal mining in England and more particularly on Alston Moor. Despite a slight setback with the dissolution of the monasteries the lead industry continued to flourish, and by the end of the 17th century it stood ready for the great leap forward in technological advancement that was the industrial revolution.

The mineral rights owners for most of the Alston Moor area, at the beginning of the 18th century, were the earls of Derwentwater. But following their disastrous involvement in the rebellion of 1715 the estates and mineral rights passed to the Crown and in 1735 were granted to the Royal Hospital for Seamen at Greenwich, better known as the Greenwich Hospital. It was under their tutelage that the area became one of the chief centres for technological advancement of the lead industry for the next two centuries.

The other factor of crucial importance for the area was the granting in 1692 of a charter to "The Governor and Company for Smelting Down Lead with Pittcoale and Seacole". This later became known as the London Lead Company and after 1704 the Quaker Lead Company, becoming the largest single employer of men on Alston Moor until the end of the 19th century. The company operated from two bases, Nenthead and Garrigill, but it should be remembered that it also had interests in other areas of England and Wales. It is important to note that the company's original charter makes no mention of getting ore but is only concerned with smelting. However, it was a small step from smelting to placing the company in a position from where it could also control the supply to keep the mills working.

Before the London Lead Company began to systematically work the Alston Moor area, most of the mining had been carried out in an extremely piecemeal way by small companies or individuals who could not afford to develop the mines to their full potential. However, by 1780 the mines under the control of the company were completely modernised and were brought together under a single system of development and working.

The London Lead Company leased the mines from the Greenwich Hospital for a duty of one-fifth or one-sixth of the ore actually produced. Initially, they then sold the ore back to the mining companies for smelting but by 1767 the commissioners of the Hospital decided to smelt their own and built a mill at Langley, where they were close to coal supplies. The fall in the price of lead in the 19th century led to reductions in duty paid as low as one-ninth.

The Greenwich Hospital commissioners appointed two receivers in the area to oversee the mining and smelting activities and to ensure that the Hospital's mines were being worked efficiently. Perhaps the two most famous receivers worked in the 1770s and were responsible for one of the greatest engineering projects in the area. In 1775 Richard Walton and John Smeaton reported to the Hospital commissioners that a drainage level should be driven from Alston to Nenthead, with the purpose of draining existing mines and also exploring and hopefully locating new mineral veins at depth. The route eventually chosen followed the course of the River Nent and the tunnel driving commenced in July 1776, the tunnel eventually being nine feet square and nearly five miles long. The Nent Force Level, as it was known, was built so large in order to act as a canal with which to bring out the spoil (waste rock) created by the tunnelling. The canal went as far as Nentsberry Haggs Shaft, some three miles from its entrance, where a massive "step" of about 160 feet was created before the level continued of normal proportions to its end at the Brewery Shaft in Nenthead. The level became something of a tourist attraction and Sopwith (1833) described a journey along it.

It is navigated by boats 30 ft in length, which are propelled in four feet water by means of sticks projecting from the sides of the level; and thus may be enjoyed the singular novelty of sailing a few miles underground, and beholding with perfect safety the various rocks that it passes through ... The hanging rocks suspended over the entrance with the Romantic scenery adjoining, and the neighbouring waterfall, renders a visit, even to the exterior, highly interesting; but this is much increased by a subterranean excursion ... The old and sometimes grotesque dresses worn on such occasions add to the mirth and cheerfulness which prevail - while the fine effect of vocal or instrumental music, and the exercise of propelling the boat, add to the singular feeling which is excited by so bold an adventure.

Regrettably for so magnificent a venture, the Nent Force Level discovered only one new vein to justify the £80,000 that it cost and the sixty-six years it took to complete.

The London Lead Company continued its involvement with Alston Moor and was in the forefront of many of the changes affecting the mining and metallurgical industry all through the 18th and 19th centuries. Indeed, many new inventions sprang from the area, such as Pattinson's smelting techniques, Attwood's slime trunking machine, and Brunton's continuous cloth separator. The London Lead Company was without doubt one of the most successful companies to have operated anywhere in Britain, but in 1882 it put its Alston Moor operation up for sale. Unlike most companies it did this while still making consistent profits, but the continuing slide in the price of lead throughout the latter half of the 19th century meant that profits were decreasing.

The debt which the area owes to the London Lead Company is considerable for not only was it involved in mining and smelting but also in every other aspect of life in the North Pennines. It sponsored schools, brass bands, chapels, sporting events and welfare services. But why this apparent altruism? Hunt (1970) explains it thus:

Efficient management meant controlling the labour force at home as well as at work, and educating the next generation into a proper sense of discipline.

The way in which companies paid their miners in the North Pennines deserves an explanation as they did not just earn a basic wage. The bargain system operated in the area, described by Forster (1821) as:

The miners take a piece of ground, commonly called a length in which they propose to raise ore ... according to the richness of the mine or working. A length of ground is commonly either twelve, fifteen or twenty fathoms, and the price of procuring the Ore, depends much upon the hardness, the expense of drawing the Stone or Ore out of the Mine, and the probable quantity of metal that can be raised.

The bargain system did not just end with the getting

of the ore, Sopwith (1833) writes:

> The bargain usually includes not only the labour in the mine, but also for gunpowder and candles, for the conveyance of the stone or ore, & etc. to the day or outside of the mine, and also for the washing and preparing it as to be fit for smelting. It is by the bing of 8 cwt of ore, that the price of working is fixed.

This system meant that the mine owners were getting quite a good deal - payment by results. This system could be extended to almost any underground occupation so that shaft sinking and level driving could all be "bargained" per yard. The only occupations paid a weekly wage were surface workers such as blacksmiths and smelter operatives. Naturally, setting the bargains needed a high degree of skill on both sides. The mine owners' agent had to know the mine well in order not to set the pay too high, while the miners had to have an excellent knowledge of both general mining and the particular place concerned so as not to set their price too low. Sopwith (1833) makes the point:

> It may easily be perceived how much it is in the interest of the working miner to be well acquainted with the various appearances in strata and veins, that he may judge of and make his bargains accordingly. Hence a spirit of enquiry is created, which naturally extends to other subjects, and the miners generally possess a degree of shrewdness and intelligence rarely found in a labouring class of people.

The bargain system continued to the end of the London Lead Company's reign, in 1882, although it had changed greatly and the miners had become virtual wage-earners.

The London Lead Company sold its entire holding in mines and mills to the Tynedale and Nent Head Zinc Company for £30,562.7s.6d (Raistrick, 1977) and moved the centre of operations to Middleton in Teesdale. Regrettably, during this time the new company did little new development and this, coupled with a plunge in the price of lead and zinc, forced the company to sell its assets in 1896.

The buyer was a Belgian company, the Vieille Montagne Zinc Company, with substantial interests elsewhere in Britain, especially in Wales. It continued development around Nenthead and was responsible for many technical innovations, not least the incredible use of air and water at the Brewery Shaft near the smelt mill. In 1910, following a fire which destroyed the old mill, a new mill was built (the remains of which are still there, in use as a bus garage), at the time the most up to date in the country. This was followed by development work in the Nentsberry Haggs Level, including the sinking of the 415 ft deep Wellhope Shaft which was working from 1923 to 1938 and produced over 250,000 tons of rough ore (Raistrick & Jennings, 1965). The company also developed the Rotherhope Fell Mine and these ventures, along with some reworking of spoil, enabled the company to keep in operation until 1949.

The leases were then taken up by Anglo-Austral Mines Ltd who began to rework the spoil for fluorspar as well as developing the mines at Nentsberry for zinc production - though little was ever processed. This company had relinquished the lease by December 1961 and following this, despite the lease being taken on several occasions, the area has remained idle.

This idleness has been to the advantage of some, namely the modern mine explorer. The mines around Alston Moor offer a richness of industrial archaeology rarely equalled in any other part of Britain.

The underground workings are characterised by two peculiarities which set them apart from other areas in Cumbria. The first is the way in which the tunnels and levels are often stone arched, and this has contributed to the way in which the underground environment has survived so well. This stone arching is all the more remarkable in that the stone was often quarried outside and trammed into the mine. Secondly, the ore often occurs not in the more familiar veins but in massive "flats", described in 1833 by Sopwith:

The ore in these flats (as the name implies) lies horizontally, and the excavations in them are several yards in breadth... Flats occasionally reach to great extent like a regular stratum, and terminate suddenly by a back or joint in the strata, and not in a wedge-like shape.

It is hard to predict the future of the Alston Moor area for it is virtually certain that mineral veins remain which may yield enough ore to make their exploitation commercially viable. Time alone will tell.

Greenside Lead Mine, Lakeland's deepest, richest, and most extensive mineral venture, high in the fells above Glenridding, Ullswater. Greenside, as well as being a producer of silver and one of the biggest employers in the area, was a pioneer in the use of electricity. The first underground electric winding motors and the first electric locos ever to be used in a British metalliferous mine saw service at Greenside, powered by electricity generated from hydro-electric plant on site.

There were three main underground shafts in Greenside, besides a number of secondary shafts and sumps. One of the earliest was Willie Shaft, sunk on the Low Horse Level and powered by hydraulic engines with water brought from flooded workings behind the dams of the High Horse Level. Lucy Shaft, on Lucy Tongue Level, was also equipped with hydraulic engines while Smith Shaft, located on Warsop Crosscut, a branch of the Lucy Tongue Level, boasted the first electric winding motors in a British metal mine.

The Willie Shaft, sunk from the Low Horse Level during the 1850s, drew the water for its hydraulic engines from flooded workings behind the dams of the High Horse and Glencoyne levels. The penstock valve in the picture is sited behind the main High Horse Level dam at the head of a rise, down which the pipes plummet. The dams were breached during the 1930s, long after the hydraulic engines became redundant, to provide a means of escape via the Glencoyne Level in the event of an accident.
(photo, Ian Matheson)

Water pipes descending the rise from the High Horse Level to the Low Horse, a distance of 240 feet. Installation of the pipes must have been a major feat of engineering in itself. Once on the Low Horse Level the pipe heads in the direction of the Willie Shaft but soon disappears in the collapses of the Great Stope. The ladders in the rise were installed during the 1930s when the mine inspector insisted on a second route of egress from the mine, the Lucy Tongue being the only route to the surface at that time. *(photo, Ian Matheson)*

Pinned between the walls of the rise, the hydraulic feed pipe is as secure today as it was on its installation.
(photo, Alen McFadzean)

Deeper and deeper into the depths of Greenside. In the lower section of the rise between the High and Low levels, the wooden ladders give way to cumbersome chain ladders which swing alarmingly in the confines of the narrow shaft.
(photo, Ian Matheson)

Reinforced girder roof in the Low Horse Level, directly beneath the Great Stope, one of the huge 19th century workings on the Greenside Vein. Metal reinforcing of this kind is rare in Lakeland mines. No doubt the company decided the added expense was necessary as the Low Horse Level was part of the emergency exit to Glencoynedale.
(photo, Alen McFadzean)

Ore hoppers in the stopes of the Alma ore-shoot, midway between the Low Horse Level and Lucy Tongue Level. The stopes of the Alma were up to forty feet wide in places, and ascended hundreds of feet, from the Lucy Tongue Level, through the tough Borrowdale volcanic rock to the floor of the Low Horse. Here in the Alma the hoppers were ranged alternately on either side of the tunnel to take advantage of the wide workings immediately overhead. *(photo, Ian Matheson)*

A hopper stands in a sub-level of the Alma ore-shoot. Tubs were run under the hoppers then filled with veinstone blasted from the stope above. Note the kibble standing between the tramlines. This is made from a length of rubber conveyer belt, strapped together with iron bands. It was used for winching tools and explosives from the Lucy Tongue Level to the workings of the Alma. *(photo, Ian Matheson)*

Iron ladder and compressed-air pipes ascending a rise in the Alma workings, Greenside Mine. *(photo, Ian Matheson)*

The Alma Level, worked between 1937 and 1961, was the main haulage road in the Alma ore-shoot. Driven along the vein, two-hundred feet above the Lucy Tongue Level, ore from the stopes above was loaded into tubs, run to the end of the tunnel, then tipped into a second stope to fall clattering to the hoppers on the Lucy Tongue. The black strands hanging from the timber in the roof of the level are the stems of a rare fungus. Until quite recently the fungus formed a heavy curtain across the level, making passage uncomfortable and more than a little eerie.
(photo, Ian Matheson)

A side-tipping tub in the Alma stopes, loaded with rock from the hoppers and waiting to discharge its cargo to the hoppers on the Lucy Tongue Level, over two-hundred feet below. It has been waiting, poised on the lip of the drop, since 1961. *(photo, Alen McFadzean)*

The signalling hammer at the head of the ladderway from the Lucy Tongue Level to the Alma illustrates that even in the depths of a Lakeland lead mine technological advancement recognises no bounds. Equipment, tools, and probably dynamite, were hauled up the rise by a compressed-air winch bolted to the staging at the side of the manhole. The signalling hammer was controlled by a wire running down the rise to the main level below.

Frozen in time - a place for the miners to sit and have their bait. Thirty years have passed since the tool boxes were used and the rubber pipe hissed with air from the compressors at the head of Smith Shaft.
(Ian Matheson & Alen McFadzean)

Warsop Crosscut, driven at right angles and in both directions, off the Lucy Tongue Level, connects the foot of Willie Shaft with the head of Smith Shaft. Greenside's original underground electrical plant was situated in the crosscut and fed by cables brought along the Low Horse Level and down the Willie Shaft. In 1912 the entire electrical installation was modernised, power being brought into the mine along the Lucy Level. *(photo, Mike Mitchell)*

In a chamber off Warsop Crosscut lie the concrete foundation beds where the 500 cfm Alley McLellan air-compressor was situated. Powered by electricity brought in from the surface plant, the compressor provided air for the rock-drills, winches, and other underground machinery. The walls of the chamber were whitewashed to maximise the available light. Behind the block wall in the corner, Warsop Crosscut continues to the foot of Willie Shaft, which was abandoned after timbers collapsed and stripped the entire shaft. *(photo, Mike Mitchell)*

Excavations on the old mill site beneath the High Horse Level in June 1980 led to the unearthing of a 19th century buddle. The buddle was a device for separating pulverised veinstone into its various minerals. The fine veinstone was shovelled onto the conical centre where water, fed from a pipe, and a paddle system, agitated the mixture and gradually distributed it across the floor, leaving the heavier galena particles near the centre and washing the waste to the edges. Waste ducts from the buddle delivered the water to the beck. The tips in the background, waste from the High Horse workings, form part of Top Dam. *(photo, Alen McFadzean)*

Goldscope Mine, in the Newlands Valley, has been worked since the 15th century for copper and since the 19th for lead. *(photo, Chris Jones)*

The East-West Crosscourse, a galena-bearing vein in the Borrowdale volcanic rocks of Helvellyn, was exploited for forty years at Wythburn Mine, above Thirlmere. The crosscourse can be seen as a band of pale mineral striking into the roof of No.1 Level. The vein is mostly quartz with a little barytes, and carries an inch thick rib of galena at this point. Wythburn Mine was worked from the late 1830s to the 1880s, though never made a profit.
(photo, Alen McFadzean)

A bleak winter morning in the bouse teams outside Smallcleugh Mine, Nenthead, in the North Pennines. Here, ore was tipped from the mine and reloaded into wagons to be taken by horse to the smelter.

The Assay House and office of the London Lead Company at Nenthead. *(photo, Chris Jones)*

A stone arched tunnel in Brownley Hill Mine, Nenthead. Stone arches are a feature of the Pennine mines - one thing that makes them remarkable is that, in most instances, the stone was quarried outside and brought in specifically for the purpose. Note the double sets of tramlines. The set on the right was a siding for tubs being loaded from the ore hopper, while the set on the left was a loop for through traffic.
(photo, Sheila & Anton Thomas)

Dynamite became available during the 1870s and has been used in a multitude of forms and for a multitude of purposes ever since. The early varieties were based on a mixture of nitro-glycerine and kieselguhr, a diatomaceous earth. Other variants were nitro-glycerine and sand (which became unstable in water), and nitro-glycerine and gun cotton, which was probably the case in the picture above. The term "powder" is still used in today's coal industry and covers a range of explosive materials, much the same as the word "dynamite" is still used in the slate quarries when referring to blasting gelatines. The metal boxes beneath the dynamite packages contained No.6 detonators. The picture was taken in Carr's Mine, Nenthead. *(photo, Mike Mitchell)*

All that glitters is galena, the common ore of lead. Here, in an ore-flat in the depths of Smallcleugh Mine, there is ore in plenty for the enthusiastic collector.

Not all of the Pennine galena was won by relative ease from horse levels such as Smallcleugh. A few hundred yards to the west of the Smallcleugh portal, and within the village of Nenthead, lies the entrance to Rampgill Mine. The Rampgill horse level intersects the Brewery Shaft, a concrete-lined abyss which descends over three-hundred feet from the surface to workshops and equipment chambers on the Nent Force Level.
(photos, Alen McFadzean & Mike Mitchell)

COAL

by Ronnie Calvin RM

The Cumberland coalfield extends along the coast from Whitehaven to Maryport, a distance of fourteen miles, and varies in width from four to six miles. From Maryport it continues a further twelve miles to Wigton but narrows to about two miles in width. A large area of coal has been worked under the sea bed, from Flimby down to Whitehaven. But it is in the Whitehaven area that the majority of undersea mining has taken place, with the coal being mined up to four miles out from the coast. The first coal mine in Cumbria to work the undersea coal was Saltom Pit.

There are seven principal coal seams in the Whitehaven area.
- Upper Metal Band - 3 ft 6 ins wide - 48 fathoms deep (at Wellington Pit).
- Preston Isle Yard (Burnt) - 2 ft 6 ins wide - 53 fathoms deep.
- Bannock - 6 ft wide - 74 fathoms deep.
- Main Prior - 9 ft wide - 96 fathoms deep.
- Little Main - 2 ft wide - 127 fathoms deep.
- Six Quarters - 6 ft wide - 139 fathoms deep.
- Four Feet - 2 ft 3 ins wide - 187 fathoms deep.

The dip, or direction of downward slope, of all the above seams is seaward, with a fall of approximately 1:2. The Main seam crops out near the line of the low road to St Bees, and has been worked from a very early period along the outcrop as far as Partis Pit, near Stanley Pond, Mirehouse. The Bannock Seam crops out at a correspondingly higher level. At first the coal was worked from the outcrops where the seam was exposed. Work began around 1620. The miners dug the coal, then women and girls carried it out in baskets on their backs. These early workings were known in the Whitehaven area as bearmouths, and a bearmouth roadway into the old workings still exists, just off the end of Pottery Road. This particular bearmouth was linked to Wellington Pit, then ran on to Haig Pit, William Pit, and Lowca Pit. It was last reopened in March 1989 when gas was found to be penetrating into the houses on Low Road, Whitehaven. The area shaft team broke into the old bearmouth drift in order to install a ventilation chimney to draw the gas away.

One of the earliest records of coal mining in West Cumberland dates to 1560 when Sir Thomas Chaloner, lord of the manor of St Bees, in granting certain leases within the manor, reserved for himself the right to dig for coals, while at the same time granting his lessees liberty to take coals from his pits, for their own use, on the condition that they paid and laboured from time to time therein, according to the custom of the manor.

The Lowthers came on the scene in 1600 when Thomas Wybergh mortgaged the manor of St Bees to George Lowther, the eighth son of Sir Christopher Lowther. Gerard, the second son, then declared an interest.

Next the eldest brother, Sir John, became the possessor and transferred his title to his second son, Christopher, who was the founder of the Whitehaven branch of the Lowther family.

Sir Christopher Lowther died in 1644 and was succeeded by his infant son, John. On reaching manhood Sir John began to take the greatest possible personal interest in the extension of Whitehaven's trade and the development of the coal mines. Indeed, he may be truly described as the founder of the Whitehaven collieries, which were worked by the Lowthers - ably assisted by their agents, the Speddings - till August 1888, when the working pits and a large tract of submarine coal were leased to the Whitehaven Colliery Company. Thus the mines stayed in private hands till the industry was nationalised in 1947.

A major development in coal mining took place in West Cumberland about 1650, when to win new tracts of coal pits were sunk and drifts cut horizontally from the lower grounds to drain the workings. This arrangement was called the pit and adit system. The coal was originally raised by jackrolls and later by horse gins.

In 1663 Sir John Lowther drove a long level from Pow Beck near the copperas works in Ginns. This was driven in a westerly direction under Monkwray and into the Bannock Seam. The level drained an area sufficient to serve the needs of the coal trade until nearly the close of the 17th century. On the 10th of November 1715, in order to win coal from deeper levels, Lowther installed the first steam pumping engine in a Cumberland mine, at Stone Pit, Howgill, near Whitehaven. The engine, a Newcomen engine with a 17 inch cylinder, was hired for £182 per annum.

Another great feat took place in in West Cumberland in 1729. The Lowthers started sinking Saltom Pit, right on the sea shore, just clear of the cliffs. The sinking of this new mine, so close to the sea and to work the coal under the sea bed, was quoted as being the most remarkable colliery enterprise of its day. When the pit had been sunk 252 feet a strong blower of gas was pricked, then piped to the pit top where it burned for many years. The agent, Mr Spedding, offered to supply the gas to the town of Whitehaven but the trustees did not take up his offer. But from an adjacent pit the gas was pumped to the laboratory of Dr William Brownridge, an eminent scientist who lived in Whitehaven, where it was used to heat his furnaces.

Throughout their history the coal mines of West Cumberland, and in particular those in the Whitehaven area, were plagued with firedamp (CH_4), and as greater depths were reached the problem of ventilation became critical. Accumulations of gas precipitated explosions which killed or maimed the colliers and seriously damaged the underground workings. One of the earliest of these explosions happened at Priestgill Colliery, in 1682, killing one miner and injuring six more. To the employer, the damage done to the mines was more important than the loss of life.

New methods of lighting and ventilation were tried. One of the most important of the early inventions was the Spedding steel mill, the first attempt to produce a safe means of lighting in an atmosphere containing firedamp. This new device was merely a steel disc fixed to a small cogwheel and geared to a larger wheel. When the handle was turned a piece of flint was held against the disc, creating a stream of sparks which enabled the miners to see to work.

The use of the Spedding steel mills spread throughout the north of England. They were used till the introduction of the Davy lamp in 1819. A fine example of a steel mill is on display in Whitehaven Museum.

But still the terrible carnage to women, boys, girls, and colliers, took place on a regular basis. The rescue of the miners and the fighting of the underground fires were left to the miners and agents. The owners played a very small part in rescue, their main concern being the damage and how much money they would lose. Early rescue workers were untrained; just ordinary workmen willing to give their lives, sometimes in vain attempts to rescue trapped workmates. As methods progressed a few specially trained workmen were, from time to time, called on to rescue miners, fight underground fires, and recover bodies.

These trained men gave a very valuable service but it was not until the 20th century that the first fully trained west Cumberland rescue team was set up at Brigham.

The first Coal Mines Act was introduced in 1842, forbidding the employment of women underground. On the 10th of August 1850 the Act for the inspection of coal mines received the royal assent. It provided for the appointment of inspectors and the official registration of all mine accidents. These first inspectors had very little power and no qualifications. The penalties for mine owners who breached the regulations under the 1855 Act was a fine of £5 with an additional fine of £1 per day until the law was complied with. Offending colliers, however, might be imprisoned for up to three months.

In 1851 the Royal School of Mines was set up to train the inspectors, but it was not until 1872 that real progress was made. The Act made it compulsory for all mine managers to pass a Government examination of competence - this is now called the 1st Class Ticket.

The first mines inspector for Cumberland was Matthis Dunn, who was appointed in November 1850. He also had to inspect collieries in Northumberland, Durham, and Scotland - which did not leave much time to inspect the Cumberland mines. The last resident inspector was Mr Stephen, a gentleman who was always willing to give help and advice on all aspects of mine safety. After he left in 1983 the county's mines were covered by visiting inspectors, Mr Vincent and Mr Armstrong, the latter being a former resident inspector who was familiar with the gas and geological problems of the coalfield.

Wooden props were the main means of supporting coal workings but at the pit bottoms - and main haulage roads and junctions - brick walls were built and roofed in timber, second-hand steel, and old tramlines. The timbers used in the Whitehaven mines of 1750 were imported from Norway by Sir James Lowther. There was a large number of these "Noraways", as they were called locally, in the old Wellington workings, up by Saltom Drift off Haig No.5 coal road. Some of these timbers are still supporting the old workings, and pre-date Haig's sinking (1911). Some of the large 24 inch square head setts up at the old junctions were still as good as the day they were set. And if you were lucky enough to be near repair work in some of these old places, the off cuts made great kindling wood for the fire.

Wood was also used for break blocks on winders and haulages. The railway poplar trees (*poplus* and *Euramericana regenerata*) from the Penrith area, were planted when the railway authorities altered the route of the London to Glasgow line in the 1880s. The requirement was that each butt had to be at least 30 inches through and more than 10 feet in length, clear of branching. The last tree from this local source was supplied to the Cumbrian colliers in 1979 by Mr John Hird, the timber merchant. A local landowner has planted more in case they are required at some time in the future.

Although there is a wealth of information to be found on the Alston area, and specifically on the lead mining industry, there is a paucity of material about coal mining. The most comprehensive source is the *Victoria County History*, but even there the bias is towards the West Cumberland coalfields rather than East Cumberland.

According to the *Victoria County History* the first record of an early attempt to prove coal in East Cumberland is in the books of the Newcastle Corporation wherein it is stated that in 1552 coal was bored for in Greenside Rigg in the parish of Farlam. However, Bouch claims, in *Prelates and People of the Lake Counties*, that the Dacre family worked the mines at Tindale Fell before 1485.

The earliest collieries were found mainly in the valleys of the Black, Hartley, and Haining burns, at

Thirwell, Tarnhouse Colliery (Tindale Fell), Talkin and Brampton, and during the 19th century at Croglin, Blenkinsop, and Lambley in Northumberland. Harris says, in *Cumberland and Westmorland Transactions 1974*, that the Carlisle Papers (at the Department of Palaeography and Diplomatic of the University of Durham) contain a wealth of information about the mining history of East Cumberland. They refer particularly to output, royalties, and the rise and decline of collieries, but also include information about colliery farms, small-holdings, and the character of settlements generally within the mining areas.

With regard to Alston, the first known source appears to be M Jars in 1765, who described in his book *Voyages Metallurgiques* the Crow Coal in the mountains of Alston Moor as being unfit for the forge, but excellent for burning lime. *Jollies' Directory* from 1811 mentions that Alston produces lead ore and coal, but gives no details. *Parson and White's Directory* from 1829 describes the Crow Coal as "containing a large portion of pyrites, burns very slowly, but is intensely hot, with very little flame, and emits a strong smell of sulphur. It is found in thin seams near the surface and is used by the miners, who mix it with clay, and make it up into balls for the fire". Subsequent directories merely repeat this information.

The major area of mining activity (at least as documented) appears to have been Tindale Fell where there were many pits. In 1801 Tarnhouse, on Tindale Fell, and Talkin Collieries, produced 197,015 loads of coal. The output rose to 278,615 loads in 1810. The drifts then at work were William, Morpeth, Fox, George, and Henry.

From early times coal had been worked at other places from the carboniferous limestone series along the Pennine range, but apparently it was mainly used for lime burning. The most important area of such mining was said to have been at Croglin. When the manor of Croglin was purchased by Charles, Duke of Somerset, in 1738, it included a colliery which was in continuous operation till 1864.

There were also early coal workings at Hartside and Renwick in the Crossfell range, the earliest reference being in the account book of Lady Anne Clifford, 1665.

Payed for Pitt Colls for my Howfs heare att Brougham Castle - Payed the 2: Day [May 1665] to John Unthank of Culgart and others for 50 loads of Pittcoals for my house here at Broughm Castle brought from Hartshead in Cumberland at 1^s per load two pounds and ten shillinges.

In 1900 the *Victoria County History* lists forty-three collieries in Cumberland, three of which were at Alston and one at Nenthead. These were:
- Alston Drift Colliery, owned by W Benson, with fifteen employees
- Guttergill Colliery, owned by Vieille Montagne Zinc Co, with seven employees

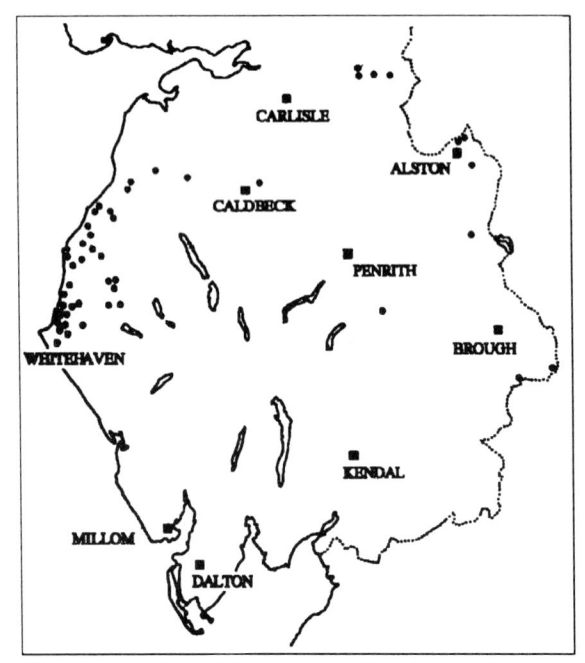

The general disposition of coal mines in Cumbria

- Rock Hill Colliery, the Alston and Nentforce Limestone Quarry Co, with six employees
- Dowgang Colliery, Vieille Montagne Co, seven employees.

In 1905 these firms were the only producers of coal at Alston and did not employ more than forty persons underground in the aggregate. The three firms were all working the little limestone coal which in the Alston district is found in two distinct seams, twenty feet apart, the upper being about twenty inches thick and the lower twelve inches thick.

The total number employed in 1900 in the collieries was 8,646, the great majority of whom were in the West Cumberland coalfields. When put in this context the Alston collieries must be seen as very small.

The Cumbria Sites and Monuments Record shows mine-related sites at Blagill (NY7347), Hesleywell (NY7547), Rotherhope Fell (NY7142), Nenthead (NY7844), Garrigill (NY7544), Crossgill (NY7441), and Middle Fell (NY7388, NY7443). This information has been picked up from 1st edition Ordnance Survey maps and contains no details of the various sites. However, according to R Fairburn, the Nenthead levels which were driven to exploit the Coalcleugh coal were worked by a small group of miners from 1840 to 1940 (SMR5911).

Aside from the records at Durham University, it may well be that company records for Vieille Montagne Co and the others mentioned above are in existence and could prove useful. Also, the NCB may have an archive or early material.

Coal has also been worked on a small scale in the Caldbeck, Shap, and Stainmoor areas. At Caldbeck, the little limestone coal crops out on the southern flanks of Warnfell Fell, and numerous shafts indicate that the seam has been extensively worked. Its thickness is said the vary between 1 foot and 2.5 feet. A lot of this coal would have been used for lime burning.

T Eastwood makes reference to a plan dated 1847 showing workings in the little limestone coal, north-east of the Denton fault belt, and the waterwheel and steam engine pits of Denton Holme Colliery, situated near Sebergham church. This coal was said to have been 20 inches thick at a depth of 160 feet in the waterwheel shaft.

Coal was also worked in the limestone near Paddigill. Again this was thin coals associated with the limestone. If you study the place names around Sebergham you will see that lime burning was carried out in this area - Kiln Gate and Lime Kiln Nook, for example. There are still a lot of old lime kilns marked on the Ordnance Survey maps.

Coal was worked on a small scale between Sleagill and Reagill, near Shap. To this day there are two fields called Pit Hills. It was also worked on a small scale at many localities in the lower carboniferous series at Borrowdale, Stainmoor, and in the westphalian Argill coalfield. Mining on Stainmoor dates from an early period, as the account book of Lady Anne Clifford illustrates:

Payed for Stainmor pitt coals for my Howfs heare at Brough Castle in Westmorland - Payd the 22nd Day [December 1665] to Robt Barret for 120 loads of Pitt Coals for my houfe hear att Brough Castle in Westmorland at 10^d a load, ffive pounds.

Coal was worked by adits on the north bank of Argill Beck, where it was said to have been nearly 4 feet thick. A trial pit was sunk in 1946 in Argill Beck and 2 feet of coal, overlain by siltstone, was proved. The last small coal working in this area was an adit, now collapsed, where coal up to 7 feet thick was said to have been worked. Mining ceased in 1946.

Looking out to sea along the No.5 coal road in the Haig Pit, Cumbria's last deep coal mine, November 1982. The road was modernised to facilitate FSVs, the free steering vehicles which were lowered down the main shaft prior to closure. *(photo, Ronnie Calvin)*

Junction below the deputy station at the bottom of Quinn's Drift, Haig Pit, November 1982. The cross-drift leads to the bottom of No.1 Drift, while the tunnel in the centre leads to Old Rigg's pump lodge. *(photo, Ronnie Calvin)*

Testing for gas with a Davy lamp prior to entering Quinn's Drift, during salvage work in the Upper Metal Band. Note the ventilation doors and the rope haulage. *(photo, Ronnie Calvin)*

Pit deputy Ronnie Calvin, Davy lamp on his belt, inspecting a mona pump at Rigg's pump lodge, down in the depths of the Haig Pit. The Haig Pit was considered to be a dry mine, despite the fact the main coal faces were several miles out under the Irish Sea. *(photo Ronnie Calvin)*

Down on the shore beneath the Haig Pit is the appropriately named Beach Drift. Water from the depths of the pit was pumped up No.4 Shaft to run out into the sea along the drift. The Beach Drift enters No.4 Shaft about 200 ft below the shaft top. *(photo, Ronnie Calvin)*

Whitehaven has been a thriving port since ancient times, and its sea defences illustrate its past importance to the Cumbrian economy. Despite the fact countless thousands of tons of iron ore and coal have been loaded from its quays it is best remembered for the humiliating attack it suffered at the hands of Captain John Paul Jones during the American War of Independence. In recent years the town has seen a marked decline in its maritime tradition. Within the last ten years the railway sidings and the coal loading facilities have disappeared - though the sand below the harbour wall is still black with Cumbrian coal. Here, the Ballyrory, one of the the last coal boats to steam out of Whitehaven harbour laden with coal from the Haig Pit, heads out for the Irish Sea.   *(photo, Ronnie Calvin)*

Brass bands and clear skies to mark the death of the Cumbrian deep coal mining industry. The last shift at Haig Pit marches out through the gates and towards the town of Whitehaven. Work ceased on the last longwall face, the 240, on the 25th of May 1984, bringing production to a halt. On Monday the 18th of November 1985 salvage work began in the underground workings and on Friday the 17th of January 1986 all the underground fans were stopped. On the 27th of January the mine manager took the last underground ride to pay a visit to the stopping behind which are entombed fourteen miners, killed in explosions in 1927 and 1928. By Friday the 17th of February 1986, all of Haig's shafts had been sealed with concrete. *(photo, Ronnie Calvin)*

The union banner, depicting the William Pit, sunk in 1808, and photographed at the commemoration service on the 27th of March 1986.

Some of these men had travelled a long way to be at this service for Haig was still a part of them, as it was the centre of all our lives. The service was a simple but moving one. You could see the strain on the faces of the gathering as it progressed, but the miners of Haig would have one last go. All the colliers past and present formed up to proudly walk out of the pit yard for the last time. Carrying the last pit banner through the centre of Kells and on down the hill to the recreation ground, they were accompanied by the town band.

As the procession passed the rows of houses, groups of people were gathered; most of these people had connections with Haig. So it was a quiet wave to the miners as they passed by. So ended a very sad day. If you take a walk down town you don't see the groups of miners standing chatting in the market place anymore. But now and then you bump into an old workmate and the talk is about the weather or "Have you found work yet?". Still a lot of them say: "Why did they close Haig? There is still plenty of coal down there".   (quotation and photo, Ronnie Calvin)

Clarghyll Colliery, a private drift mine in the north Pennines, is sited below the main Alston to Hexham road, about a mile outside Alston. It started producing coal in 1940 and is still working the same levels. There are two levels, or drifts, serving the mine. One is the main return airway and the other the intake roadway which is used for access and haulage. This main intake road twists and turns its way for over a mile into the main coal face area.

The method of working the coal is by shortwall or gate and stall. Small roadways are driven off at right-angles to the main roadway. These, in turn, are split into ten-yard stalls, with one miner to a stall taking five yards of coal from each side of his gate road. The photograph shows empty coal tubs being hauled in along the main access level. *(photo, Ronnie Calvin)*

The seam, one of the narrowest ever worked in the county, varies in thickness from 17 inches to a "good height" of 21 inches. The miners fill their own tubs, which they identify with a token. Each miner is paid by the tubfull, each tub holding eight hundred-weights of anthracite coal. They trail their own tubs out of their gate roads, over a set of flat sheets, then on to the main haulage road. Sets of eight or twelve tubs are then winched out to surface by the main haulage, sited on the fell. *(photo, Ronnie Calvin)*

Getting stuck in. All the coal is won by hand, the miner using a windy-pick to break the mineral down. He lies flat or on his side, holding the back of the machine in both hands. No stone is taken out of the face - just coal - so the working height is determined by the thickness (or the thinness) of the seam. Even in the trailing and haulage roads, only enough stone is blasted out to give sufficient clearance for a fully laden tub. *(photo, Ronnie Calvin)*

BARYTES

by Alen McFadzean & Ian Tyler

Unlike copper, lead, iron and coal, the common minerals of the county, barytes has been mined as a commercial product only since recent times. Prior to the mid 18th century it was of little value to the mining companies and was, along with calcite, quartz, and other gangue minerals, thrown over the tips as a waste material. Nowadays barytes is in great demand for a variety of purposes and the Lake District mines have, in recent decades, produced many thousands of tons. Lakeland's barytes industry, though, terminated in 1990. when Force Crag - the last working mine - was forced to close after a serious collapse in the main adit level brought production to a halt. Mining still continues on a small scale in the Cumbrian Pennines, where the mineral is worked from an opencast at Silverband Mine.

Barytes (barium sulphate, $BaSO_4$), or barite as it is sometimes called, varies in colour from a bluish-yellow to brown and red. It has a glassy lustre, is usually opaque, and commonly comprises tabular, equidimensional crystals, in masses or featherlike formations. It often forms the gangue material of sulphide ore veins - which is how it occurs locally - though in sedimentary rocks it manifests as nodules and free-growing crystals.

Some of the finest barytes specimens ever discovered have come from the mining fields of Cumbria. Single crystals, some of them eight inches in length, have been won from the local mines. But the mineral occurs in a variety of forms throughout the world. Near Norman, Oklahoma, barytes is found in the form of desert roses and in perfect imitation of the flower; while near Stirling, Colorado, it occurs as blue crystals in the local sediments. In Rumania, in the mines of the Felsobanya region, barytes occurs as flat, yellowish crystals intermingled with stibnite. It has been mined extensively in Europe, where it is found in association with other minerals, notably sphalerite.

Perfect crystals of barytes have been discovered in association with sphalerite in the lower levels of Force Crag Mine, Coledale, near Keswick. Here the mineral forms the vein material, but in the course of mining many large natural cavities, or vugs, have been discovered, the walls of which have been adorned with splendid specimens. In the mines of Alston, transparent crystals have been found, though more commonly barytes occurs locally as a pale, featureless mineral resembling gypsum, felspar and calcite, from which it can be determined by hardness and weight. Indeed, it was in regard to the latter characteristic, with a specific gravity of 4.48, the miners christened it "heavy spar".

Its uses in today's chemical industry are manifold. It is added to paint products as a lead substitute and forms a pigment in the preparation of lithopone. Barytes mud is used extensively in the oil exploration industry where it adds weight to the special drilling lubricants in deep boreholes. It is mixed with concrete in the construction of nuclear installations, and provides the substance of a barium meal for internal x-rays. It has been, and still is, used as a filler in the cloth and paper industries; and if local tradition is to be relied on, has been mixed with flour by the miserly millers of Braithwaite.

Mines in which barytes has been present as a vein ore, and worked as a commercial mineral, include Blencathra Mine, Ruthwaite Mine, Potts Gill Mine, Sandbeds Mine, Force Crag Mine, and the mines of the Cross Fell area. Barytes has also been present as gangue mineral in Greenside and Hartsop Hall mines, in Patterdale, and at Wythburn Mine, Thirlmere.

Force Crag has been one of the main producers, though when the mine was first investigated in 1755 it was galena - the mineral ore of lead - not barytes that proved to be the attraction. It was to be some time, over a hundred years in fact, before the gleaming white spar was to command its own market - as Postlethwaite, writing in 1889 in his *Mines and Mining in the English Lake District*, illustrates.

> The deposits of sulphate barytes which occur in the Force Crag vein are amongst the most remarkable mineral deposits that have been found in the Skiddaw slates; they commonly measure from three to five feet in thickness, and one was found in 1872 which measured ten feet in thickness. Some of the barytes is very pure and white; but a great deal is coloured by the psilomelane with which it is associated, and with iron.
>
> The psilomelane also occurs in considerable quantities, but very little of it can be obtained in a pure state.
>
> The mine was opened up, or probably reopened, by Mr Walton of Alston, and Messrs Dowthwaite & Cowper, of Keswick, and others, about eighty years ago; there is no definite information on this point, but the author can remember that in the year 1846 [sic - 1848] some of the proprietors had become tired of their enterprise and the mine was stopped three months in order that the company might be wound up, and a fresh lease taken out in the names of those who were prepared to carry on the work, which they did for about thirty years, and succeeded in raising a large quantity of ore.
>
> Messrs Walton & Co paid very little attention to the barytes, as it was scarcely saleable during the greater part of their tenure; but in later years it has been more extensively used in the manufacture of plate glass, and for the more questionable purpose of adulterating white lead, consequently the mineral has been in greater demand.
>
> After a short interval of inactivity the mine was taken up again by a company of local gentlemen, for the purpose of raising barytes. They commenced operations in the low level, but afterwards discovered that the mineral was much more plentiful higher up the mountain; therefore, the old mine was abandoned, and two more levels were driven still higher up the mountain, and large deposits of barytes discovered.

And so, like the majority of Lakeland mines, Force Crag's history developed as a series of intensive working periods and interludes of abandonment. The upper reaches of the mine, High Force, situated above the 2,000 ft contour on the steep slopes of Grisedale Pike, were worked exclusively for barytes, the galena and sphalerite being extracted from the lower levels of the mine. Today, several decades after the upper mine was abandoned, it's still possible to examine the worked out stopes and study the techniques employed by the barytes miners of yesteryear.

The main vein at Force Crag is vertical by nature though dips slightly to the north. It has been worked by a series of levels driven from the fellside, intersecting the mineral over a series of heights. As with most Lakeland mineral mines, once the levels had been driven they were then linked internally by a series of shafts and ladderways, to aid the extraction of the mineral and facilitate the movement of men and equipment from one level to another.

One of the interesting features of the Lakeland barytes mines, which puts them apart from the other mineral workings, is the wide adoption of the pillar system. The veins were stoped away leaving huge blocks of mineral in situ to enhance the stability of the mine. In some areas of Force Crag, and particularly in High Force, the pillars have been robbed, leaving parts of the mine in a dangerous condition. Many pillars still remain, spanning the dark stopes with broad sections of gleaming white and yellow barytes, allowing an insight into the richness and impressive width of the barytes veins.

Mineral was removed from the veins with high explosives. Once dislodged it was allowed to lie in the floor of the stope prior to being drawn off from the tramming level below through wooden hoppers. Again, most mineral mines used hoppers in this manner, though the barytes industry appears to have been particularly suited to this mode of extraction. Extensive batteries of wooden hoppers were built in the tramming levels of Potts Gill and Sandbeds, the rich barytes mines of the Caldbeck fells. And in High Force the batteries of the 1100 ft Level, and the miniature hoppers in the narrow 650 ft Level, emphasise the fact that not only was mining an industry for skilled and knowledgeable men of the rock, it also encouraged the craft of woodworking and allowed no end of scope for creative genius.

In the upper levels of High Force stand a pair of wooden towers, wedged firmly between the walls of the stope but resembling those transportable siege towers of medieval Europe. They were built by craftsmen during the early years of the 20th century to act as manways between tramming levels. At one time, and particularly during periods of activity, they would have been access routes when the walls of the original internal shafts had been robbed away and the stopes were lying deep in mineral waiting to be drawn off from below. Now the stopes are empty, robbed of their mineral. The hoppers have been drawn and the towers stand alone - monuments to the men who made them.

Similar wooden structures, known as mills, were erected in the Caldbeck barytes mines. In certain instances, where the ore was extracted by the "cut and fill" method, these wooden ore-passes were built above the hoppers as the stopes gradually filled with waste material. One obvious advantage of this method of working was that dead rock could be stacked underground. Blasted veinstone was sorted where it fell, the ore being thrown down the mill, the waste left in the floor of the stope. As the roof of the stope ascended and the waste deepened, the mills were extended. This technique was employed at several locations in the county, notably the Threlkeld lead mines, and in the mines of the Alston area. In most instances the mills were constructed of masonry for added strength and many superb examples still exist in the north Pennine ore-fields. Locally, there are masonry-lined mills in the far reaches of Force Crag's No.1 Level and in the vein workings of Rachel Wood lead mine at Thornthwaite.

Caldbeck was the other main barytes mining area of the Lake District fells. Situated in a two-mile area of decomposed Borrowdale volcanic rock on the north side of High Pike, the barytes lodes course across the fell in an east-west direction, cutting the many copper and lead veins for which the Caldbeck fells are famous. Mining started in earnest in the 19th century, though undoubtedly the Elizabethan miners were aware of the existence of the beautiful heavy spar.

The main barytes producers were situated within the complex of workings between Fell Side and Calebrack. Old Potts Gill, and the ground around Sandbeds, Potts Gill, and Deerhills, was opened as early as 1844, but the venture was not a success. A second attempt in the 1880s by the Cleator Moor Iron Company also failed to make any headway. Ruthwaite Mine, at Ireby, was first worked in 1869 and produced ore intermittently, under various companies, into the 20th century. But it was not until hard times swept the country during the lean years of the Great War that the barytes situation, generally, started to improve.

The Potts Gill mines worked on and off till the 1940s, when prospects were good for the Caldbeck fells and barytes mining took off in a big way. Driggith Mine, which had produced copper and lead, had been reopened for barytes in 1926 but came under new ownership no less than three times during the 1940s. East Potts Gill Mine commenced in 1942, and soon mineral was being produced from the Back Vein where barytes formed a rib a full six feet in width. The outcrop of Sandbeds East was discovered in 1927 but exploration and production did not proceed till 1946. Sandbeds West Mine, which was a continuation of the lodes worked in Sandbeds East, was not discovered till 1956.

The veins varied in width from a few inches to twenty feet, though not all the filling was barytes. The main gangue mineral was quartz, with barytes averaging a thickness of just under two feet. Some 150,000 tons of dressed barytes were produced from the mines of Caldbeck. Operations ceased in 1966 with the closure of the Sandbeds mines.

East Cumbria

There have also been trials and small barytes mines in the outlying areas of the Lake District, such as at Gilcrux and Ireby, near Cockermouth. Barytes mining, though, developed into a sizeable industry in the eastern borders of the county. The western slopes of the Pennine hills have numerous steep-sided valleys, created during the ice ages by glacial action which revealed the mineral veins.

The mined area commences in the north at Hartside and follows the escarpment down through the Hilton and Appleby area to Brough. No less than fourteen major veins have been worked for lead, barytes, witherite and fluorspar. Many of the mines are to be found at the inhospitable region where Cross Fell and Dun Fell dominate the area. Here wind speed averages 50 to 60 MPH.

A feature of the local barytes formation is that it forms in tabular translucent crystals. One of the largest ever discovered, mined at Dufton, weighed nearly a hundred-weight and is now on display at the Geological Museum.

Mining started in this area during the 14th century. The veins were hushed to expose them at depth or worked by bell pits, with water drained off by adits. The London Lead Company worked the whole of this area from 1820 to 1880, exclusively for lead. Then interest in barytes increased and the area once again became active.

Hartside Mine is situated on the northern side of the Hartside Pass. The vein was first worked commercially for barytes by the Hedworth Barium Company. After the initial investigation the mine was taken over by the La Porte Company who invested quite heavily, developing the Harrison Level and laying an inclined tramway from the adit to the road. The barytes was then taken to the company mill at Silverband, some ten miles to the south. La Porte worked the mine from 1940 to 1946, during which time they produced 15,000 tons of dressed barytes.

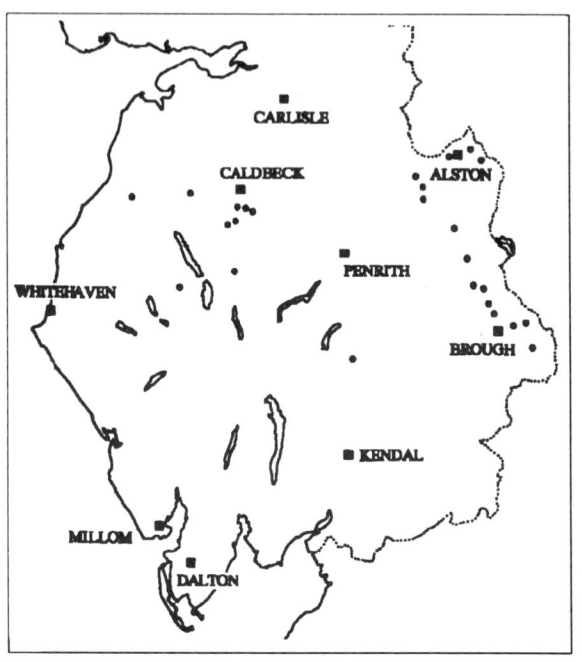

The general disposition of barytes mines in Cumbria

Just below the summit of Dun Fell is to be found Silverband Mine, the last working mine in the western Pennines, and now encompassed by a nature reserve. Originally worked for galena by the London Lead Company, the first contemporary company was again La Porte, who worked the mine extensively for barytes, and between 1839 and 1963 produced a staggering 215,000 tons of dressed ore.

The mine, situated at an altitude of over 2,000 feet, presented the company with a transportation problem. This was solved by the erection of an aerial ropeway, three-and-a-half miles down to the plant, the remains of which are still visible. Much of the equipment was dismantled on La Porte's directions and the mine became derelict.

In 1970 the lease was acquired by H Taylor, who worked the mine with great vigour and produced 75,000 tons of barytes. In 1983 the mine came under the auspices of Cragg & Curtiss Ltd, who are now working high above the mill and opencasting the vein. The ore is milled on site then transported down the steep winding road in huge lorries to the valley below.

Just a few miles to the south of Silverband is the picturesque village of Dufton, whose rows of neat red sandstone cottages and manorial hall bear witness to more prosperous times. Three miles up the winding track Dufton Mine is to be found between the 2,000 and 2,300 ft contours. Like most of the mines in this area, Dufton Mine was originally worked by the London Lead Company until they shut it down in 1873.

One of the main adits was Atkinson's Level, which produced both lead and barytes. Between 1882 and 1899 the mine was worked exclusively for barytes, some 9,500 tons being produced. A little work was done during the 1914-18 war but in more recent times a company took the lease and worked the mine dumps, the mill processing some 200 tons per week until 1986. The lease was then taken over by Nor-West Holst Ltd in 1987, who worked the veins high on the fell by the opencast method. But the project was shelved more or less overnight and the workings landscaped. The site suffered badly and the original London Lead Company buildings, along with most of the modern plant, were buried.

Still further south, towards Appleby, lie the ancient mines of Hilton and Murton. Prior to the London Lead Company workings, 1824-1876, records indicate mining activity as early as the 14th century.

Barytes was mined when the Scordale Mining Company took the lease in 1896. In the first year of operation 70 tons of witherite were produced. At the end of their tenure, in 1906, the lease was taken by the Brough Baryte Company Ltd, who worked till 1912. The total barytes production between 1896 and 1912 was 7,194 tons.

The Scordale company took the lease again and worked till 1919 when the mine fell idle. The mine was taken over - for the last time - by Messrs W Wharton in 1930, who worked till 1939. Surprisingly, La Porte, who were working various other mines in the area, took out the lease but never actually mined any ore.

The dramatically beautiful Force Crag, a vertical wall of rock at the head of Coledale, a narrow valley near Keswick. The name "Force", a common place name element in Cumbria, is derived from the Scandinavian word *foss*, meaning waterfall. The huge tips from Force Crag Mine's No.3 Level dominate the middle ground, while in the foreground stand the mill and mine office. High Force Mine, being the upper workings of Force Crag, and to which the lower workings were connected underground by the La Porte Incline, was situated on the high slopes of Grisedale Pike, beyond the ridge of the crag. A surface road to High Force ran off to the left of the picture and skirted along the top of the crag. *(photo, Alastair Cameron)*

Boring the barytes vein in the 1500 Stope on Force Crag's Zero Level. Force Crag was the last working mine in the Lakeland fells and was forced to close during 1990 when a serious collapse blocked the Zero Level.

Connecting the long-delay detonators in the 1500 Stope. The shot-holes have been charged with 80% blasting gelatine and are nearly ready for firing. Note the rib of solid barytes in the centre of the vein.
(photos Ronnie Calvin)

After the shot has been fired the ventilation pipe is run in to the stope and the poisonous fumes sucked away. The blasted veinstone has fallen into the hopper chutes but some of the larger lumps need to be reduced further. Here, barytes chips fly through the air as a 14lb hammer, wielded by miner Peter Calvin, does the business. *(photo, Ronnie Calvin)*

Down on the Zero Level, beneath the hoppers under the 1500 Stope in Force Crag Mine. Miner Peter Calvin and New Coledale Mining Co executive, Lindsay Greenbank, filling an ore tub with veinstone. *(photo, Ronnie Calvin)*

The most northerly slopes of the most northerly fells in the Lake District lie bleak and bare. Here, in days gone by, John Peel hunted the fox in his "Coat sae grey". The Elizabethan miners roamed these fells in search of copper and lead - but the deep scars radiating from Potts Gill, cutting Deer Hills and High Pike, date from relatively modern times. The Caldbeck barytes mining industry flourished in the 1940s and 1950s, but ended in 1966 with the closure of Sandbeds Mine. But the mines are far from silent. Subsidence still occurs for the veins were worked to the subsoil, the miners leaving only a few feet of ground between the stope roofs and the grass. Landslips are common and deep holes have a habit of appearing without warning. *(photo, Alen McFadzean)*

Abandonment in the fells above Potts Gill, Caldbeck. Here a shaft from one of the Potts Gill workings stands derelict and dangerous. The shaft has since collapsed. All dangerous subsidence craters and open shafts in the Caldbeck fells are now securely fenced.
(photo, Dave Bridge)

A collapse on a barytes vein on the northern flank of High Pike. The rotten nature of the country rock is well illustrated in this picture. Also in evidence is the barytes vein itself. The vein has been removed to within three feet of the surface but the miners left a pillar of barytes about fifteen feet down. *(photo, Alen McFadzean)*

Not only is the instability of the ground in evidence on the surface - subsidence has devastated the underground ramifications of the Potts Gill mines and left vast areas inaccessible. Here, on the Blockley Vein, the wooden roof has been swept away and the tramming level blocked. The collapse probably occurred through a hopper. The ore tub on the left of the picture has been lifted clear of the rails and jammed against the wall.
(photo, Alen McFadzean)

An ore tub rots away in the levels of the Blockley Vein, abandoned beneath an empty hopper. The tub is made from iron but the gate on the tipping end is made from wood. Note the long strap hinges and the draw bolt at the bottom. There is also a wooden "buffer" in the middle of the gate to prevent the draw bolt buckling when coming into contact with other tubs.
(photo, Alen McFadzean)

A barytes pillar in the Blockley Vein, Potts Gill Mine. This particular pillar is small compared to examples in High Force and areas of the Caldbeck fells. Pillars were left in situ to prevent the walls of the worked out veins buckling under pressure and collapsing into the mine.
(photo, Alen McFadzean)

A hopper in the Blockley Vein, Potts Gill Mine, Caldbeck. Many references to hoppers have been made during the course of this book, so its only fitting that some attempt should be made to explain exactly how a hopper operates. The hopper - basically a wooden chute - was constructed beneath a hole in the level roof, immediately below the floor of a stope. As the vein was worked, the floor of the stope gradually filled with blasted veinstone, which was drawn off from below through the hoppers. To fill a tub, the wooden plank across the throat of the hopper was eased up with a pinch-bar or removed altogether - depending on the size of the material coming through. More often than not, the plank would be removed and nothing would come, the material requiring a poke with a bar to get it moving. To stop the flow the plank would be inserted and knocked down with a hammer. *(photo, Alen McFadzean)*

High in the Pennines stand the remains of the aerial ropeway at Silverband Mine, installed by the La Porte Company for conveying barytes from the mine to the mill, three-and-a-half miles away and several hundred feet below.
(photo, Ian Tyler)

GLOSSARY OF MINING TERMS

ADIT - a horizontal tunnel driven into the hillside for access to the vein or to drain water from the mine.

BACK FILLING - waste rock which is dumped in a disused area of the mine to save the time and expense of bringing it out to day.

BALL MILL - revolving steel drum containing steel balls for crushing the ore.

BARGAIN SYSTEM - ritualistic system of paying miners on the amount of ore or slate raised from a predetermined section of ground; the miners worked in companies of three or more men, and the firm paid the companies as opposed to the individuals, at monthly or six-monthly intervals; this system was still being used in the Lakeland slate quarries in the 1940s.

BARYTES - or heavy spar, a sulphate of barium, mined extensively in the northern Lakes and Pennines.

BEARMOUTH - adit or level running into a hill, usually associated with coal mining.

BLACK JACK - mining term for sphalerite, the ore of zinc.

BLACK LEAD, BLACK CAWKE - Cumbrian terms for wad or graphite.

BLAST FURNACE - originally fuelled by charcoal, these furnaces were introduced to Cumbria in 1711 to produce iron from hematite ore.

BLENDE - mining term for sphalerite; see Black Jack.

BLOOMERY - a hearth, used since ancient times, and in the form of a clay dome, for processing hematite ore into workable iron.

BLOOMSMITHY - a technological advancement from the stringhearth; a modification of the latter though possessing a forge hammer powered by a waterwheel.

BOUSE TEAM - ore bin, constructed of stone, into which ore from the mine is tipped before milling.

BORING RIG - apparatus for boring large-diameter holes through rock.

BROKEN GROUND - large scale subsidence associated with iron ore mining in Furness and the West Coast.

BUDDLE - apparatus for separating ore from veinstone.

CONCENTRATES - processed ore, usually non-ferrous, suitable for smelting.

CLOG - lump of quarried slate.

CLOSEHEAD - underground quarry for the working of slate.

COFFIN LEVEL - a narrow tunnel, coffin-shaped in section, usually dating to the Elizabethan period and driven without the use of explosives.

COUNTRY ROCK - naturally occurring rock, igneous, metamorphic, or sedimentary, in which the mineral vein is situated.

CROSS-VEIN OR CROSSCOURSE - a vein running counter to the major lodes in a mine.

CROSSCUT - a tunnel driven through country rock to intersect the vein or mineral deposit.

CRUSHING ROLLS - heavy iron rollers used during the primary stages of milling.

CUT AND FILL - mining method by which a stope is mined upwards and the waste rock is left underground in the floor of the working.

DAY - underground term meaning "surface" or "outside".

DEADS - waste rock, usually stacked carefully underground to support the workings.

DIP - the angle of declination of a mineral vein or coal seam.

DRESSING - the reduction and sorting, by hand or machine, of veinstone into grades suitable for further processing; also the process of trimming roofing slates to their finished size.

DRESSING FLOOR - a cobbled area where dressing has taken place.

DRIFT - haulage or exploratory tunnel running along the vein or through mineralised ground.

FACE SHOVEL - large digger for use at the face of a quarry.
FALSE FLOOR - the floor of a tunnel made of timber and clay, constructed after the original floor has been mined away.
FATHOM - nautical measurement of six feet, widely used in the mining industry.
FEEDER (RUNNER) - an underground stream, frequently found in carboniferous limestone, and a curse to the iron miners of Furness.
FIREDAMP - explosive methane gas associated with coal mining.
FLAT - a body of ore, flat by nature, usually sandwiched between the bedding planes of sedimentary rock.
FLOTATION - a process separating the concentrated vein material by the application of oil rising through water, to which the minerals adhere.
FLOWSTONE - secondary mineralisation, forming curtains and cascades in the same manner that stalagtites are formed.
FLUE - chimney stack, built along the ground to convey poisonous fumes from the smelt mills and discharge into the atmosphere, usually on the summit of the nearest fell.
FLUME - channel for conveying water.

GALENA - a sulphide of lead and the main lead mineral occurring in Cumbria.
GANGUE - secondary minerals in a vein, usually forming the matrix in which the more valuable minerals occur.
GIN - horse-powered capstan for raising ore or coal from a shaft.
GRIZZLEY - a series of bars set at intervals to grade the ore into determined sizes.

HAULAGE ROAD - tunnel along which tubs of ore or coal are hauled, usually by mechanical means.
HEAVY SPAR - miners' term for barytes.
HEMATITE - the ore of iron.
HOPPER - a wooden chute fixed into the wall and roof of a level, through which ore is discharged to fill tubs from the workings above.
HORSE LEVEL - a major level where horses were used for hauling tubs of ore.
HUSH - a manmade gully down the side of a fell, excavated by the releasing of water from a dam; hushing was a mining method in its own right, applied to wash ore from mineral veins by the sheer force of water.

INCLINE - a tunnel driven upwards at an angle of usually thirty to fifty degrees from the horizontal; also a surface or underground tramway, constructed to raise or lower ore or slate from one plane to another, and powered by means of gravity, water, or electricity.

JACKROLL - man-powered windlass for raising kibbles from a shaft.

JIGS - machines for separating ore from waste by means of agitation.
JUMPER - hand-held drilling steel.

KIBBLE - a large iron bucket for raising ore or equipment up shafts.
KIDNEY ORE - hematite ore in its usual form.

LEATS - courses cut into the fellside, or through rock, to channel water for the operation of waterwheels and other equipment.
LEVEL - horizontal access or drainage tunnel.
LODE - mineral vein.

MILL - industrial site for the processing of ore; also an underground ore-pass, constructed through waste rock, down which ore was thrown to hoppers below.

OLD MEN - miners' term for the miners of previous generations.
OPENCAST - method of mining mineral from an open quarry as opposed to an underground mine.
OVERBURDEN - the layer of unwanted material, usually glacial in origin, overlying a mineral deposit.

PELTON WHEEL - an enclosed wheel upon the periphery of which are fastened cups or small buckets which accept a jet of pressurised water; from the drive shaft, motion is transmitted to a variety of machinery.
PENCIL ORE - hematite ore manifesting in spike-like formations.
PILLAR - portion of the vein which is left in position to support the walls of a mine.
PINNEL - fine glacial boulder clay.
PIPE - graphite deposit, roughly cylindrical in shape.
PIT - a mine generally, but usually coal or iron.
PLUMBAGO - one of the many terms for wad or graphite.
PORTAL - the entrance to a level, usually constructed from local stone.
PUMP RODS - reciprocating rods of heavy timber, sometimes referred to as pit-work, conveying motion from a waterwheel or steam engine to the pumps at the foot of a shaft.

RISE - an internal shaft, usually blasted upwards through the rock to connect with a higher level.
ROYALTY - an area of land determined by a lease; also the payment demanded by the mineral owner on every ton of ore processed by the operator.
RUN-IN - a collapse in a level.
RUNNER - see feeder.

SCREENS - sieves for grading ore particles by size.
SEAM - coal deposit, usually horizontal in nature.

SETT - a timber frame to support the roof of a level; also a mineral royalty, an area of ground stipulated in a lease.

SHAFT - a hole, usually vertical or inclined at a steep angle, up which ore is raised, and down which miners descend to reach the lower levels of a mine.

SHOT HOLE - hole bored in rock to take explosives.

SMELTER - furnace for processing copper and lead ores.

SMIT - hematite ore in a greasy form, used since ancient times for marking sheep.

SOLE - the floor of a level.

SOP - large irregular body of ore.

SPOIL - waste rock tipped on the surface.

STAGE - tunnel or working horizon.

STEMMER - copper or brass rod used for loading shot holes with explosives.

STOPE - an area of the vein that has been removed.

STOPE AND FEATHERS - also called plug or slug and feathers; a chisel sandwiched between two steel wedges, or feathers, inserted into a hole and hammered, causing the rock to split by expansion; still used today in the quarrying of slate.

STRING - a vein or rib of mineral, usually secondary to a main vein.

STRINGHEARTH - technological advancement from the bloomery; the latter with a bellows powered by a waterwheel.

SUMP - a shaft sunk in the sole of a level; also a pool at the foot of a shaft in which the pumps are situated.

TAILINGS - fine waste from the milling process.

TOP-SLICING - the method by which hematite ore is removed from a sop, involving the removal of the ore slice by slice and the controlled subsidence of the ground above.

TRIAL - exploratory tunnel or quarry.

TRIBUTER - a miner working under the tribute system - similar in many ways to the bargain system.

VEIN - mineral body, usually of a vertical or near-vertical nature, striking through the rock for great distances and for great depths.

VUG - naturally occurring cavity in a vein, usually lined with fine mineral crystals.

WAD - local term for the graphite mined in Borrowdale.

WINDER - mechanism for winding ore from a shaft.

WOLFRAM - the ore of tungsten.

BIBLIOGRAPHY

Abraham G D, "The Most Valuable Mine of Today", *The Autocar Magazine*, 1917

Adams J, *Mines of the Lake District Fells,* Dalesman, Clapham, 1988

Andrews M A, *The Birth of Europe,* BBC Books, London, 1991

Anon. "Carrock Fell, UK Tungsten Mine with an interesting history is again producing concentrates", *Mining Magazine*, London, 1977

Anon. *Coniston Mine an Unpublished Essay*, Cumbria Record Office, Barrow-in-Furness, 1858

Ashley M, *The Golden Century*, 1969

Baur J, *Minerals, Rocks and Precious Stones,* Octopus, London, 1974

Becket J V, *Coal and Tobacco*, 1981

Bland R, *Unpublished History of Coniston Coppermines,* Cumbria Records Office, Barrow-in-Furness, 1978

Bolton J, *Geological Fragments of Furness and Cartmel 1869*, 1869 (rep 1978)

Boon G C, "An early Tudor Coiner's Mould and the Working of Borrowdale Graphite", *Trans Cumberland and Westmorland Antiquarian and Archaeological Soc, Vol 76 New Series,* Kendal, 1976

Bouch C M L, *Prelates and People of the Lake Counties*, 1948

Bouch C M L and Jones G P, *The Lake Counties 1500-1830*, Manchester University Press, Manchester, 1961

Britton J, Brayley E W, *The Beauties of England and Wales Vol 3,* 1805

Brownrigg R, *Buttermere Green Slate,* unpublished notes

Budworth J (Captain), *A Fortnight's Ramble in the Lakes in Westmorland, Lancashire and Cumberland by a Rambler* (2nd ed), 1795

Bulmer, *Directory of East Cumberland*, 1884

Bulmer T, *History, Topography and Directory of Cumberland*, 1901

Burt R, Waite P, Burnley R, *Cornish Mines - Metalliferous and Associated Minerals,* University of Exeter, 1987

Burt R, Waite P and Burnley R, *The Cumberland Mineral Statistics 1845-1913,* University of Exeter, 1982

Burt R, Waite P, Burnley R, *The Lancashire and Westmorland Mineral Statistics 1845-1913*, University of Exeter, 1983

Camden W, *Britannia 1598,* trans P Holland, 1610

Cameron A D, "Honister Slate Mine", *The Mine Explorer Vol III,* Cumbria Amenity Trust, 1989

Cameron A D, *Honister Slate Mine - A field Guide,* Cumbria Amenity Trust, 1990

Campbell, "Political Survey of Britain", Hutchinson W, *The History of the County of Cumberland Vol 2,* 1794 (rep 1974)

Clough R T, *The Lead Smelting Mills of the Yorkshire Dales and North Pennines,* Clough, Keighley, 1980

Collingwood W G, "Elizabethan Keswick", *Trans Cumberland and Westmorland Antiquarian and Archaeological Soc, Series No 8,* Kendal, 1912 (rep 1987)

Collingwood W G, "Germans at Coniston in the Seventeenth Century", *Trans Cumberland and Westmorland Antiquarian and Archaeological Soc, Vol 10 New Series,* Kendal, 1910

Collingwood W G, *Lake District History,* 1925

Collingwood W G, "The Keswick and Coniston Mines in 1600 and later", *Trans Cumberland and Westmorland Antiquarian and Archaeological Soc, Vol 28 New Series,* Kendal, 1928

Collingwood W G, *The Lake Counties,* 1902, rev 1932, rev Rollinson W, 1988

Cooper M P, Stanley C J, *Minerals of the English Lake District - Caldbeck Fells,* Natural History Museum Publication, London, 1990

Crosthwaite J F, "Old Borrowdale", *Trans Cumberland Assn for the Advancement of Literature and Science,* Pt 1, 1875-76

Crosthwaite J F, "The Crosthwaite Registers", *Trans Cumberland and Westmorland Antiquarian and Archaeological Soc, Vol 2 Old*

Series, Kendal, 1874-75

Cumberland Geological Society, *Proceedings Vol 2 parts 2 and 4, 1967,* 1969-70

Cumberland Geological Society, Shipp T (ed), *The Lake District - a Field Guide,* Unwin, London, 1982

Cumbria Amenity Trust Mining History Society, *The Mine Explorer Vols 1, 2 and 3,* 1984, 1986, 1989

Cumbria Amenity Trust Mining History Society, *Newsletter No.23,* 1989

Cumbria Sites and Monuments Record

Davis R V, *Geology of Cumbria,* Dalesman, Clapham, 1979

Davies R, *John Wilkinson,* 1987

Dawson J, *Torver - The Story of a Lakeland Community,* Phillmore, 1985

Dewey H, Dines H G, "Special Reports on the Mineral Resources of Great Britain Vol 1, Tungsten and Manganese Ores", *Memoirs of the Geological Survey,* HMSO, London, 1923

Dewey H, Eastwood T, "Special Reports on the Mineral Resources of Great Britain Vol XXX", *Memoirs of the Geological Survey, HMSO,* 1925

Donald M B, *Elizabethan Copper,* 1955, Moon, Whitehaven, (rep 1989)

Dunham K C, Dines H G, "Barium Minerals in England and Wales", *Wartime Pamphlet No.46,* Geological Survey of Great Britain, London, 1945

Eastwood T, *The Lake District Mining Field - The Future of non-ferrous mining in Great Britain and Ireland,* London Institute of Mining and Metallurgy, London, 1959

Eastwood T, "Special Reports on the Mineral Resources of Great Britain Vol 22, Ores of the Lake District", *Memoirs of the Geological Survey,* HMSO, London, 1921

Eastwood T, Dixon E E L, Hollingworth S E, Smith B, "The Geology of the Workington and Whitehaven District", *Memoirs of the Geological Survey,* HMSO, 1931

Encyclopaedia Britannica, 1947

Farey J, Second Report of the Wad Mine in Borrowdale 1821 - Hunt R A, "Historical Sketch of British Mining", *British Mining Bk 1,* 1887, Stanford, London, (rep 1978)

Fell A, *The Early Iron Industry of Furness,* 1908 (rep 1968)

Ferguson R S, *A History of Cumberland,* Elliot Stock, London, 1890 (rep 1970)

Firman R J, "Epigenic Mineralisation", Moseley F, *The Geology of the Lake District,* Yorkshire Geological Society, Leeds, 1978

Forster W, *A Treatise on a section of the Strata from Newcastle upon Tyne to Crossfell,* Andrew Reid, Newcastle, 1883 (rep 1985)

Gentleman's Magazine, January 1751, Vol 21, 1751

Gentleman's Magazine, February 1751, Vol 21, 1751

Gibson A C, *Ravings and Ramblings Round Coniston,* Whittaker, London, 1849

Gilchrist D G, Moore C, "Wicham Mines, Kirksanton, Millom", *The Mine Explorer Vol 2,* Cumbria Amenity Trust, 1986

Gilpin W, *Observations relative chiefly to Picturesque Beauty made in the Year 1772 on several parts of England, particularly the Mountains and Lakes of Westmorland and Cumberland Vol 1* (2nd ed), 1778

Goodchild J G, Harkness R, *Trans Cumberland Assn for the Advancement of Literature and Science, No.8,* 1882-83

Gray T, *Journal of a Tour in the North of England,* 1769

Green W, *Guide to the Lakes Vol 2,* 1819

Harris A, *Cumberland Iron: The Story of Hodbarrow Mine,* Bradford Barton, Truro, 1970

Hatchett C, "A Tour through the Counties of England in 1796", Raistrick A (ed), *The Hatchett Diary,* 1967

Heller R L (ed), *Geology and Earth Sciences Source Book,* American Geological Institute, 1962

Hewer R E, "Bannerdale Lead Mine", *British Mining No 25,* Northern Mine Research Society, 1984

Hewer R E, "The Kelton & Knockmurton Iron Mines", *British Mining No.36,* Northern Mines Research Society, 1988

Hewer R E, "The Trials of Ennerdale Region", *British Mining Memoirs No.37,* Northern Mine Research Society, 1988

Hewer R E, "Iron Mines of Eskdale and Miterdale", *The Mine Explorer,* Cumbria Amenity Trust, 1984

Holland E G, *Coniston Copper: A History,* Cicerone, Milnthorpe, 1986

Holland E G, *Coniston Copper Mines: A Field Guide,* Cicerone, Milnthorpe, 1981

Holmes F M, *Miners and their Work Underground,* 1897

Hughes, *North Country Life in the 18th Century,* 1965

Hunt C J, *The Lead Mines of the North Pennines in the 18th and 19th Century,* Manchester University Press, 1970

Hunt I, *The Lakeland Pedlar,* Pinewood, 1974

Hunt R, "A Historical Sketch of British Mining", *British Mining Bk 1,* 1887, (rep 1978)

Hutchinson W, *The History of the County of Cumberland Vol 2,* 1794, (rep 1974)

Jars M G, *Voyages Metallurgiques Vol 2,* 1780

Jefferson, *A History of Leath Ward,* 1860

Jollie, *Directory,* 1811

Jones A, "Brewery Shaft, Nenthead", *The Mine Explorer Vol 1,* Cumbria Amenity Trust, 1983

Jones C D, "Hartside Mines", *The Mine Explorer Vol I,* Cumbria Amenity Trust, 1983

Kelly, *Directory,* 1894

Kelly, *Directory,* 1914

Larousse Encyclopaedia of Modern History, 1964

Lefebure M, *Cumberland Heritage*, Gollancz, London, 1970

Lysons, *Magna Britannia Vol 4:* Cumberland, 1816

Mannix and Whellan, *History, Gazetteer and Directory of Cumberland 1847*, (rep 1974)

Marshall J D, Davies-Shiel M, *Industrial Archaeology of the Lake Counties*, David & Charles, 1969

Marshall J D, Davies-Shiel M, *The Lake District at Work Past and Present*

McFadzean A, "Mining Methods on Lindal Moor", *UK Journal of Mines and Minerals No.6*, 1989

McFadzean A, *The Iron Moor*, Red Earth, Ulverston, 1989

McFadzean A, "The Mines of Lindal Moor", *UK Journal of Mines and Minerals No.5*, 1988

McFadzean A, *Wythburn Mine and the Lead Miners of Helvellyn*, Red Earth, Ulverston, 1987

McMahon Moore A J, "Carrock Fell Mine Cumbria", *Royal School of Mines Journal No.26*, London, 1977

Mitchell J G and Ineson P R, "Potassium-Argon Ages from the Graphite Deposits and Related Rocks of Seathwaite, Cumbria", *Proc Yorkshire Geol Soc, Vol 40, Pt 3, No 24*, 1975

Nicolson W (Bishop), "Letter to Dr Woodward, 5th Aug 1710", Nicholson J and Burn R, *The History and Antiquities of the Counties of Westmorland and Cumberland Vol 2*, 1777

Otley J, "Account of the Black Lead Mine in Borrowdale", *Memoirs, Literary and Philosophical Society of Manchester, Ser 2, Vol 3*, 1819

Otley J, *A Concise Description of the English Lakes and Adjacent Mountains (6th ed)*, Keswick, 1837

Otley J, *A Descriptive Guide to the English Lakes and Adjacent Mountains (8th ed)*, 1849

Parson W, White W, *A History, Directory and Gazetteer of Cumberland and Westmorland 1829*, (rep 1976)

Parnell J, "Genesis of the Graphite Deposits at Seathwaite in Borrowdale, Cumbria", *Geological Mag Vol 119*, 1982

Pennant T, 1772, Hutchinson W, *The History of the County of Cumberland Vol 2*, 1794, (rep 1974)

Postlethwaite J, *Mines and Mining in the English Lake District (3rd ed)*, Whitehaven, 1913, (rep 1975)

Pough A, *A Field Guide to Rocks and Minerals*, Constable, London, 1970

Prospectus for the Cumberland Black Lead Mine Company, 1859

Raistrick A, *History of Lead Mining in the Pennines*, Longmans, London, 1965

Raistrick A, *Two Centuries of Industrial Welfare*, Moorland, Hartington, 1977

Rawnsley H D, *Past and Present in the English Lakes*, 1916

Read H H, *Rutley's Elements of Mineralogy, (26th ed)*, 1970

Robinson T, *An Essay toward a Natural History of Cumberland and Westmorland*, 1709

Rollinson W, *Life and Tradition in the Lake District*, Dent, London, 1981

Sedgwick A, "Suggestions on the Origin of Plumbago", *Quart J of the Geol Soc, Vol 4*, 1848

Shackleton E H, *Lakeland Geology*, Dalesman, Clapham, (4th ed), 1973

Shaw W T, *Mining in the Lake Counties*, Dalesman, Clapham, 1972

Simonim L, *Mines and Miners*, 1868

Slater D, *Tungsten - Mineral Dossier No.5*, Mineral Resources Consultative Committee, HMSO, London, 1973

Smith B, "Iron Ores", *Special Report on the Mineral Resources of Great Britain Vol VIII*, HMSO, London, 1924 (rep 1988)

Smith B W, *The World's Great Copper Mines*, 1967

Snowdonia National Park Study Centre, Peter & Susan Crew (Ed), *Early Mining In the British Isles*, SNPSC, Plas Tan y Bulch, 1990

Sopwith T, *An Account of the Mining District of Alston Moor, Weardale and Teesdale*, Davidson, Alnwick, 1833 (rep 1984)

Strens R G J, "The Graphite Deposit of Seathwaite in Borrowdale, Cumberland", *Geol Mag, Vol 102, No 5*, 1965

Sutton S, *The Story of Borrowdale*, 1960

Tylecote R F, *A History of Metallurgy*, 1988

Tyler I, *Force Crag: The History of a Lakeland Mine*, Red Earth, Ulverston, 1990

Victory County History for Cumberland, 1905

Wallace W, *Alston Moor, Its Pastoral People, Its Mines and Miners*, Davis, Newcastle, 1986

Ward J C, "The Geology of the Northern Part of the English Lake District", *Memoir of the Geological Survey*, 1876

Weis P L, Friedman I, Gleason J P, "The Origin of Epigenetic Graphite: Evidence from Isotopes", *Geochemica et Cosmochimica Acta Vol 45*, 1981

Whellan, *History and Topography of Cumberland and Westmorland*, 1860

Williams N, "The Story of Carrock Mine", *University of Sheffield Geological Society Journal Vol 7*, 1979

Young B, *Glossary of the Minerals of the Lake District and Adjoining Areas*, British Geological Survey, Newcastle, 1987

INDEX

Alma Level, 137
Alma, the, 134 - 139
Alston, 119, 123 - 124, 151 - 153, 162, 165 - 167
Alston & Nentforce Limestone Quarry Co, 153
Alston Drift Colliery, 152
Alston Moor, 118 - 119, 122 - 126, 152
Amalgamated Industrials Ltd, 110
Angerton, 56
Anglesey, 11, 24
Anglo-Austral Mines Ltd, 125
Anotolia, 117
Appleby, 168 - 169
Armstrong, Mr (inspector), 151
Arsenopyrite, 108
Ash Gill Incline, 60
Ashburner & Son, 89
Askam-in-Furness, 88 - 90
Atkinson's Level, 169
Augsburg Co, 13, 118
Australia, 107, 117
Azurite, 11 - 12

B.30 Pit, 100, 103 - 104
B.41 Pit, 101
B.45 Pit, 100
B.47 Pit, 101, 103
Back Guards Pit, 90
Back Strings, 23
Back Vein, Potts Gill, 168

Backbarrow, 49
Backbarrow Co, 91
Backbarrow Furnace, 89, 91 - 92
Bankes, John, 43, 46, 48 - 49, 51
Bankes, Joyce, 47
Banks & Co, 50
Bann Garth Mine, 87
Bannerdale, 43
Bannock Seam, 149 - 150
Bardsey, Nicholas, 45
Bargain system, 70, 124 - 125
Barratt's Level, 17
Barratt, John, 15, 17, 26
Barret, Robt, 153
Barrow Hematite Steel Co, 89, 94 - 95
Barrow Mine, 118 - 119, 121
Barrow-in-Furness, 88, 94, 97
Barytes, 144, 165 - 169
Basinghall Mining Sdt, 120
Bate, 82, 84
Bate-holes, 76
Beach Drift, 158
Bearmouths, 149
Benson, W, 152
Bigrigg, 99
Bigrigg Mine, 86
Birkside Gill Mine, 17
Bishop Nicolson, 44, 47
Black Sal, 48
Blagill, 153
Blencathra Mine, 166

Blenkinsop, 152
Blockley Vein, 177 - 180
Bloomeries, 88
Bloomsmithies, 88 - 89
Blue Quarry, 29
Boehm, Frederick, 109
Bolivia, 107
Bolton Heads, 90
Bolton, John, 89
Bonsor Deep, or Horse, Level, 14, 17 - 19, 27, 31- 32, 35, 50
Bonsor East Shaft, 14 - 15, 19, 29, 34 - 35
Bonsor Mill, 15, 19, 25
Bonsor Vein, 13 - 15, 18, 25, 27, 29, 35, 50
Borlase, William, 119
Bornite, 12
Borrowdale, 13, 17 - 18, 43 - 46, 50, 53, 59
Borrowdale (Stainmoor), 153
Borrowdale Volcanics, 24, 29, 44, 134, 144, 167
Boss, William, 109
Braithwaite, 121, 166
Bramley Engineering Co, 73
Brampton, 152
Brandlehow Mine, 118
Brandreth, 43
Brandy Crag Quarry, 74
Brandy Gill, 108 - 109
Brewery Shaft, 124 - 125, 148

Brigham Smelter, 118
Brim Fell, 38
Bronze Age, 23 - 24
Brossen Stone Quarry, 57 - 59
Brotherswater, 118
Brough, 168
Brough Baryte Co Ltd, 169
Broughton Mills, 56
Broughton Moor Quarry, 57 - 58
Broughton-in-Furness, 89
Brown Cove, 121
Brownley Hill Mine, 146
Brownridge, Dr William, 150
Buccleuch, Duke of, 104
Bucking, 117
Buddling, 117, 142
Budworth, Captain, 49
Bull Gill Incline, 60 - 62
Burlington Slate Quarries, 57 - 58, 70, 83 - 84
Burlington, Earl of, 83
Burma, 109
Buttermere, 13
Buttermere Green Slate Co, 57
Butts Beck Mines, 89

Calcite, 117, 165
Caldbeck, 12 - 14, 107, 109, 118, 153, 174 - 175, 180
Caldbeck Fells, 118, 121, 167, 175, 179
Caldbeck Mines, 46, 167 - 168

188

Calebrack, 167
Cambourne, 107
Canada, 107
Canadian Level, 110 - 111, 116
Cann, Claude, 57
Carkettle Mine, 89
Carlisle, 122
Carn Brea, 107
Carnforth, 89
Carr's Mine, 147
Carrock End Mine, 18
Carrock Fell Mining Ltd, 110
Carrock Mine, 107, 109, 111, 114
Carrock Mines Ltd, 109
Carrock Mining Syndicate, 108 - 109, 111 - 112
Carron Foundry, 86
Cassiterite, 107
Castle-an-Dinas Mine, 107
Catal Huyuk, 117
Cathedral Cavern, 76
Catstye Cam, 120
Ceylon, 43
Chalcopyrite, 11 - 12, 21, 29
Chaloner, Thomas, 149
Charles duke of Somerset, 152
Christcliff Mine, 87
Chrysocolla, 12
Cistercians, 88
Civil War, 14, 47, 118
Clairvaux, 123
Clarghyll Colliery, 162
Cleator, Cleator Moor, 85
Cleator and Workington Junction Rly, 87
Cleator Moor Iron Co, 167
Clegg, J, 89
Clifford, Lady Anne, 152 - 153
Coal, 149 - 153
Coal Mines Acts, 151
Coalcleugh, 153
Cobblers Hole, 15, 35
Cobblers Level, 13
Cockermouth, 168
Cockermouth & Penrith Rly, 87
Cockley Beck Mine, 17
Coledale, 165, 170
Colorado, 110

Common Stage, 48
Coniston, 23, 25 - 26, 46, 56 - 59, 70, 73, 85, 88 - 89, 118, 123
Coniston Fells, 12, 21
Coniston Hall, 18
Coniston Mines, 12 - 14, 17, 19, 39, 41, 46, 50, 59
Coniston Old Man, 38, 56 - 57, 59, 72, 75
Coniston Quarries, 55, 57, 59
Conte, Nicholas Jaques, 50
Cookson, Faithful, 86
Coombe Height, 108
Coppermines Valley, 14, 25, 72
Copperplate Mine, 17
Copperplate Vein, 13
Cornwall, 89, 96, 106 - 108
Cove Quarries, 57
Crag Fell Mine, 86
Cragg & Curtiss Ltd, 169
Craig Gibson, Alexander, 15
Crete, 11
Croglin, 152
Cromwell, Oliver, 118
Crooklands Mines, 90
Cross Fell, 152, 166, 168
Cross-holes, 76
Crossfield, Stephen, 91
Crossgates, 88
Crossgill, 153
Crow Coal, 152
Crowgarth Mine, 86
Crown, the, 118, 123
Cumbrian Mining Co Ltd, 109
Cunsey Co, 93
Cunsey Furnace, 89, 91 - 93
Cuprite, 18
Cwmystwyth Mine, 11
Cyprus, 11

Dacre Family, 151
Dale Head, 60
Dalehead Mine, 12 - 13
Dalton-in-Furness, 87 - 90, 94
Davies, David, 118
Day, Charles Edwin, 42
de Merton, William, 88
Deerhills Mine, 167

Denny, J, & Co, 89
Denton Holme Colliery, 153
Derby No.1 Pit, 102, 104-105
Derby Rise, 104
Derby, Earl of, 104
Derwentwater, Earls of, 123
Devon, 107
Dissolution, the, 45
Distington, 87
Dixon's Pipe, 50
Dixon, Thomas, 48
Dixon, William, 49
Dormer, Ambrose, 45
Dow Crag, 18
Dowgang Colliery, 153
Dowthwaite & Cowper, 166
Driggith Mine, 167
Dubbs Quarry, 57
Duddon Furnace, 89, 92 - 93
Duddon Valley, 17, 56
Dufton, 168 - 169
Dufton Mine, 169
Dun Fell, 168 - 169
Dunmail Raise, 17
Dunn, Matthis, 151
Dunnerdale, 80 - 81
Durham, 151 - 153
Durham Chemicals, 110
Dutchmen, 118

Eagle Crag Mine, 24, 121
Earthquake Passage, 39
East Indies, 43
East Pool & Agar, 107
East Potts Gill Mine, 168
East-West Crosscourse, 144
Easy Gully, 18
Edward Hall & Co, 91
Edward IV, 123
Egremont, 85 - 87, 90
Egypt, 11
1100 ft Level, High Force, 167
Elizabeth I, 12, 45, 118
Elliscales, 90
Elliscales Mines, 89
Elterwater, 57, 59
Elterwater Quarries, 58
Emerson Vein, 108 - 110

Emerson, F W, 108
Ennerdale, 85 - 87, 98
Eskdale, 85 - 86
Eskdale Granite, 87
Eure Pits, 89 - 90

Falkirk, 88
Farey's Stage, 48
Farlam, 151
Fell Side, 167
Felsobanya, 165
Felspar, 165
Firedamp, 150
1st Class Ticket, 151
Fisher Quarry, 83
Fleetwith Pike, 60
Fleming's Level, 14
Fletcheras Mine, 123
Flimby, 149
Florence Pit, 90
Flotation, 118, 121
Floutern Tarn, 86 - 87
Fluorspar, 117, 125, 168
Force Crag Mine, 118, 121 - 122, 165 - 167, 170 - 171, 173
Forge Mill, 50
Four Feet Seam, 149
Fox Drift, 152
Foxfield, 18, 87
France, 123
Frizington, 87
Furness Abbey, 45, 88, 95
Furness Railway, 18, 56, 83
Furness Railway Co, 87

Gale Fell, 86 - 87
Galena, 117, 142, 144, 148, 166, 169
Garrigill, 123, 153
Gartsherrie, 86
Gate Crag Mine, 87
Gaunt's Level, 19
Gaunt, Richard, 15
Geological Museum, 168
George Drift, 152
George I, 149
Germany, 12, 118
Gilbert's Stage, 50, 54

189

Gilcrux, 168
Gill Force Mine, 87
Gill Stage, 48
Gillbrow Mines, 89
Ginns, 150
Glen Strathfarrar, 43
Glencoyne Level, 119, 121, 129
Glencoynedale, 133
Glenridding, 120, 127
God's Blessing, 13
Goldscope Mine, 12 - 14, 17, 20 - 21, 46, 118, 143
Gorton's Pipe, 45
Gorton's Stage, 48
Gorton, James, 48
Grainsgill, 107 - 108, 111
Grand Pipe, 45 - 46, 49 - 50, 52
Grange in Borrowdale, 13
Graphite, 43 - 47, 49 - 50
Grasmere, 85, 118
Great Crosscourse, 27
Great Deed of Borrowdale, 46
Great Gable, 43
Great Opening, 49
Great Ormes Head, 11, 24
Great Stope, the, 130, 133
Great War, 19, 57, 109, 121, 167
Greenburn Mine, 14
Greenhead Gill Mine, 118
Greenodd, 56
Greenside Mine, 119, 122, 127 - 128, 132, 136, 140, 166
Greenside Mining Co, 119
Greenside Rigg, 151
Greenside Vein, 133
Greenwich Hospital, 123
Grey Crag, 25, 38
Grey Knotts, 43
Grisdale's Pipe, 50
Grisedale Pike, 49, 166, 170
Guttergill Colliery, 152
Guttersby No.3 Pit, 99
Gypsum, 165

Hadrian's Wall, 122
Haig Pit, 149, 151, 154 - 155, 157 - 161
Hannay, Richard, 94

Harding Level, 109 - 110, 116
Harding Vein, 108 - 112, 116
Harding, James, 109
Harrington, 86
Harrison Level, 168
Harrison's Stage, 48
Harrison, Ainslie & Co, 89, 91, 93, 104
Hartside, 152, 168
Hartside Mine, 168
Hartsop Mine, 118 - 119, 121, 166
Hasting's Pipe, 50
Haug, Langnaur & Co, 113, 118
Haverigg, 88
Haverslack Hill, 89
Hawes Water, 17
Hawtrey, Ralph, 47
Heavy Spar, 165
Hedworth Barium Co, 168
Helvellyn, 118, 120, 144
Hematite, 85 - 90
Henning Valley, 90, 103
Henry Drift, 152
Henry III, 12
Henry VIII, 45, 123
Hesk Fell Mine, 17
Hesleywell, 153
Hetherington, William, 48
Hexham, 162
High Dam, Greenside, 121
High Fellside Quarry, 58
High Force Mine, 121 - 122, 166 - 167, 170, 179
High Haume, 89 - 90
High Horse Level, Greenside, 128 - 130, 132, 142
High Pike, 167, 174, 176
Hilton, 168 - 169
Hird, John, 151
Höchstetter, Daniel, 12, 20, 45, 47, 123
Höchstetter, Daniel(jnr), 45
Höchstetter, Emanuel, 45, 47
Höchstetter, Joseph, 47
Hodbarrow, 88, 90
Hodbarrow Mine, 90
Hodge Close Quarry, 57 - 59, 70, 77

Hoegstre, Joachim, 123
Holland, 44
Holywath, 26
Honister Crag, 56, 59 - 60, 62 - 63
Honister Hause, 59, 61
Honister Quarries, 55
Honister Vein, 60 - 62, 66 - 67
Howgill, 150
Hunter Quarry, 83

Iran, 11
Ireby, 167 - 168
Ireland, 14
Irish Row, 25
Iron Yeat, 88
Italy, 46

Jackson, James, 110
James I, 46
Japan, 58
Jigging, 17, 117
John Fell & Co, 42
Jones, Captain John Paul, 159

Kalcher, Steffan, 46
Kalcher, Thomas, 46
Kells, 161
Kelton & Knockmurton Mines, 86 - 87
Kelton Fell (loco), 88
Kendal, 49, 56
Kennedy Bros, 89
Kentmere Quarries, 56 - 57
Keppel Cove, 119 - 121
Kernal Crag, 25
Keswick, 12 - 14, 18, 43, 45 - 47, 49 - 50, 112, 118, 123, 165 - 166, 170
Keswick Journal, 13
Kidney Ore, 85
Kieselguhr, 147
Kiln Gate, 153
Kimberley Vein, 60 - 61
Kirkby-in-Furness, 55 - 58, 70, 76, 83 - 87
Kirkland, 87 - 88
Kirkstone Pass, 57 - 58
Kirkstone Quarries, 57

Knockmurton, 87
Knockmurton Mine - see Kelton and Knockmurton Mines
Korea, 107, 110

La Porte Chemical Co, 122, 168 - 169, 181
La Porte Incline, 122, 170
Ladyman, John, 49
Lakeland Green Slate & Stone Co, 57
Lambley, 152
Lamplugh, William, 46 - 47
Lancaster Canal, 56
Langdale, 57 - 58, 85
Langdale Pikes, 12
Langhorn, 86
Langley, 123
le Fleming, Anne, 14
Legh, Thomas, 45
Leicester M Hutchinson & Co, 108
Leighton Furnace, 89, 92
Levers Water, 13, 19, 23, 25, 70
Levers Water Mine, 15, 19
Lime Kiln Nook, 153
Linarite, 13
Lindal, 88, 90, 106
Lindal Cote Mines, 89 - 90
Lindal Moor, 90, 101, 103
Lindal Moor Main Vein, 100 - 101, 103
Lindal Moor Mines, 89, 106
Link Level, 61
Little Langdale, 14
Little Langdale Quarries, 76
Little Main Seam, 149
Liverpool, 121
Logan Beck Mine, 17
London Lead Co, 119, 123 - 125, 145, 168 - 169
Longsleddale Quarries, 55
Longwork, the, 13, 22
Lord Quarry, 83
Low Brandy Crag Quarry, 58 - 59, 73
Low Horse Level, Greenside, 119, 128-130, 132-134, 140
Low Scawdell, 18

Low Water, 15, 19, 74
Low Water Quarry, 72
Lowca Pit, 149
Lowther, Christopher, 149
Lowther, Christopher II, 150
Lowther, George, 149
Lowther, Gerard, 149
Lowther, James, 151
Lowther, John, 150
Lowther, John II, 150
Lowwood Furnace, 89, 92
Lucy Shaft, 128
Lucy Tongue Gill, 119 - 121
Lucy Tongue Level, 119 - 121, 128, 130, 137 - 140

Macclesfield Co, 14
Machel, John, 91
Magnetite, 18
Maiden Moor, 13
Main Prior Seam, 149
Malachite, 11 - 12, 18
Mandall's Slate Co, 57
Manesty Vein, 13
Margaret Mine, 90
Marron, 87
Marton, 88 - 89, 100, 102, 105 - 106
Maryport, 121, 149
Maryport Carlisle Rly, 87
McAlpines, 67
McKechnie Bros, 122
Merchant Adventurers, 46
Mesopotamia, 11
Mexico, 43
Mexico Mine, 13
Michaelangelo Schl of Art, 46
Middle Fell, 153
Middle Level, Paddy End, 37 - 38
Millom, 85, 88
Millom & Askam Hematite Iron Co, 104
Mills, 167
Mines Royal, 12 - 13, 45 - 46, 118
Ministry of Supply, 109 - 110
Minworth, 111
Mirehouse, 149
Monkey Shelf, the, 60

Monkwray, 150
Moor Field, 102
Moor Stage, 48
Morpeth Drift, 152
Mosedale Beck, 87
Mosedale Quarry, 56 - 57
Moses' Trod, 56
Moss Bay, 86
Moss Head Quarry, 59, 72 - 73, 75
Moss Rigg Quarry, 57, 59
Mouzell, 88, 90

Nab Gill Mine, 87
Nag Beck Incline, 60
Napoeonic Wars, 49 - 50
Napoleon I, 50
National Carbonising Co (Energy) Ltd, 110
Nationalisation, 150
NCB, 153
Neilsons of Glasgow, 88
Nent Force Level, 124, 148
Nenthead, 123 - 125, 145, 147 - 148, 152 - 153
Nentsberry Haggs Level, 125
Nentsberry Haggs Shaft, 124
New Coledale Mining Co, 122, 173
New Engine Shaft, 15, 19, 27
New England, 43
Newcastle-on-Tyne, 46-47. 119
Newhouse Gill, 43, 48
Newland Furnace, 92 - 93
Newlands Valley, 12 - 13, 22, 46, 118, 121, 143
Newton, Isaac, 47
Nibthwaite, 18, 56
Nibthwaite Furnace, 89, 92
Nitro-glycerine, 147
No.1 Level, Force Crag, 167
No.1 Level, Wythburn, 144
No.3 Level, Force Crag, 170
No.4 Shaft, Haig, 158
Non-Ferrous Minerals Development Ltd, 109
Nor-West Holst Ltd, 169
Norman Conquest, 122
Norman, Oklahoma, 165

North Stank, 90
Northumberland, 151 - 152

Old Engine Shaft, 15, 18 - 19, 27 - 32, 34
Old Hills Mines, 89
Old Man Quarries, 70
Old Men's Stage, 46 - 50, 52
Old Peru - see B.30 Pit
Old Potts Gill Mine, 167
Old Rigg's Pump Lodge, 155
Orgrave, 88

Paddigill, 153
Paddy End, 73
Paddy End Mine, 14 - 15, 18 - 19, 25, 27, 36 - 37, 70
Paddy End Old Vein, 36
Park, 90, 94
Park Mines, 89 - 90
Partis Pit, 149
Parys Mountain, 11
Patterdale, 24, 119, 166
Peel, John, 174
Pencil Ore, 85
Pennington, 88
Penny Level, 109
Pennybridge Furnace, 89, 92
Penrith, 107, 109, 151
Penzance, 108
Pit Hills, 153
Plumbago, 43
Plumpton, 88
Portugal, 107
Potts Gill Mine, 166 - 167, 174 - 175, 177, 179 - 180
Pow Beck, 150
Preston Isle Yard Seam, 149
Priestgill Colliery, 150
Primrose Pit - see Stank No.7 Pit
Psilomelane, 166
Pyrites, 152

Quaker Lead Co, 123
Quartz, 117, 144, 165, 168
Quinn's Drift, 155 - 156

Rachel Wood Mine, 167

Rake Vein, 50
Rampgill Mine, 148
Ravenglass, 56
Ravenglass & Eskdale Rly, 86 - 87
Rawlinson Shaft, 102
Rawlinson, J, 89
Rawlinson, William, 91
Reagill, 153
Red Dell, 27, 29
Red Gill Mine, 13, 18, 87, 118
Red Tarn, Helvellyn, 119, 121
Redmond, 16
Redruth, 107
Renwick, 152
Ricket Hills Mines, 89
Rigg Head Quarry, 57
Roanhead, 88, 90
Roanhead Mines, 90
Robertson Research International Ltd, 110
Robinson, Thomas, 47
Robson's Level, 50
Robson's Stage, 53
Rock Hill Colliery, 153
Roe, Charles, 14 - 15
Romans, 12, 55, 86, 117 - 118, 122
Rosthwaite, 59
Rotherhope Fell, 153
Rotherhope Fell Mine, 125
Rotterdam, 123
Roughtongill Mine, 13, 17-18, 118 - 119
Rowrah, 87
Royal School of Mines, 151
Rumania, 165
Ruthwaite Mine, 166 - 167
Rydal Estates, 14

Saddlestone Quarry, 59, 72 - 73
Sadgill Quarry, 55
St Austell, 107
St Bees, 149
St Bees Sandstone, 85
St Thomas' Work, 13
Saltom Drift, 151
Saltom Pit, 149 - 150
Saltwell Mine, 13
Sandbeds East Mine, 168

Sandbeds Mine, 166 - 168, 174
Sandbeds West Mine, 168
Sandside, 56
Saudi Arabia, 58
Scafell, 12
Scald Cop Quarry, 72
Scale Beck, 86
Scale Beck Mine, 87
Scheele, K W, 43
Scheelite, 107 - 108
Schneider, Henry William, 94
Scneider, Hannay & Co, 89-90
Scordale Mining Co, 169
Seathwaite, 43, 46 - 47, 49, 80
Seathwaite Tarn Mine, 17
Seatoller, 43, 45, 48 - 49
Sebergham, 153
Sellafield, 87
Shap, 153
Shaw, Willie, 35
Shepheard, John, 47
Siberia, 43
Silicosis, 96
Silver, 117 - 122
Silver Gill Mine, 13
Silverband Mine, 165, 168 - 169, 181
650 ft Level, High Force, 167
Six Quarters Seam, 149
68 yrd Level, Derby Pit, 105
Skelwith Bridge, 58
Skiddaw Granite, 107
Skiddaw Slate, 12, 20, 44, 85 - 86, 88, 108, 120, 166
Sleagill, 153
Smallcleugh Mine, 145, 148
Smeaton, John, 124
Smith Shaft, 120, 128, 139 - 140
Smith Vein, 108, 116
Smithy Hill Quarry, 83
South Crofty, 107
South Cumberland Iron Co, 87
Spain, 43, 90, 117, 122
Spanish Pioneers, 109
Specular Ore, 85
Spedding, Matt, 77
Spedding, Mr, 150
Sphalerite, 117, 165 - 166

Spion Kop Quarry, 59, 72, 75
Spout Crag Quarry, 58
Stainmoor, 153
Stainton, 88, 90
Stainton Mines, 90
Stang, the, 119
Stank, 88, 94
Stank Mines, 90
Stank No.1 Pit, 95 - 97
Stank No.2 Pit, 95
Stank No.5 Pit, 95
Stank No.7 Pit, 94
Stell, John, 45
Stephen's Vein, 36
Stephen, Mr (inspector), 151
Stibnite, 165
Sticks Pass, 119 - 120
Stirling, Colorado, 165
Stirlingshire, 86
Stone Anvils, 24
Stone Close, 90
Stone Pit, 150
Stoneycroft Mine, 118
Stringhearths, 88 - 89
Swaledale, 48

Talkin, 152
Tampimex Oil Products, 121
Tar, George, 58
Tarnhouse, 152
Tarnhouse Colliery, 152
Taylor's Level, 19, 33
Taylor, H, 169
Taylor, John, 14 - 15, 27, 29, 50
Tenorite, 18
Thirlmere, 144, 166
Thirwell, 152
Thornthwaite, 167
Thornthwaite Grange, 109, 112
Thornthwaite Mine, 109, 118 - 119, 121
Threlkeld Mine, 109, 118, 167
Thurland, Thomas, 12
Tilberthwaite, 57 - 58, 78 - 79
Tilberthwaite Gill, 70
Tilberthwaite Mine, 14, 17, 48
Tilberthwaite Quarries, 56, 58
Tincroft, 107

Tindale Fell, 151 - 152
Top Dam, Greenside, 120
Top Height, B.30 Pit, 100, 106
Top Level, Greenside, 119
Top Level, Paddy End, 19, 36, 38 - 41
Top Slicing, 90
Torver, 57, 59
Town Quarry, 83
Triddle Mine, 15
Triddle Shaft, 15
Troutbeck, 119
Tynedale & Nent Head Zinc Co, 125

Ullswater, 127
Ulpha Mine, 17
Ulverston, 85, 88 - 89
Ulverston Canal, 18, 56
Ulverston Mining Co, 89 - 90
United States, 58, 107, 110, 117
Unthank, John, 152
Upper Metal Band, 149, 156
Urswick, 88, 90

Vale of Lorton, 87
Vieille Montagne Zinc Co, 125, 152
Vincent, Mr (inspector), 151

Wad, 43 - 50
Wadham, Mr, 90
Wadhole Gill, 48
Walna Scar Quarries, 56 - 57, 80 - 81
Walton & Co, 166
Walton, Richard, 124
Warnfell Fell, 153
Warsop Crosscut, 128, 140 - 141
Warsop, Thomas, 42
Wasdale Head, 56
Waste, the, 100 - 101
Waterfall Vein, 110
Waterhead, 56
WECO Development Corp, 110
Wellhope Shaft, 125
Wellington Pit, 149, 151
Wetherlam, 17, 27, 29, 42, 73

Wetherlam Mine, 42
Wharton, W, 169
Whinfield, 90
Whinfield Mines, 89
Whitehaven, 85 - 87, 99, 149 -151, 159 - 160
Whitehaven Colliery Co, 150
Whitehaven Iron Mines Ltd, 87
Whites of Widnes, 61, 73
Whitmore & Vernon, 46
Whitriggs, 94
Whitriggs Gin Pit - see B.30 Pit
Whitriggs Mines, 89 - 90
Wicham Mine, 90
Wicham Valley, 88
Wickersley's Sop, 49
Widnes, 122
Wigton, 149
Wilkinson, Isaac, 49
William Baird & Co, 86 - 87
William Drift, 152
William Pit, 149, 161
Willie Shaft, 119, 128 - 130, 140 - 141
Wilson Vein, 110
Wilson, Captain Anthony, 109, 112
Wilson, J D, 110
Wilson, William, 109
Windermere, 89, 91, 93
Winkle's Pipe, 50
Witherite, 168 - 169
Wolfram, 107 - 110
Woodbine Pit, 90
Woodman's Pipe, 45
World War II, 57 - 58, 121
World Wide Energy UK Ltd, 110
Wrengill Quarry, 56 - 57
Wybergh, Thomas, 149
Wythburn Mine, 121, 144, 166

Yarlside, 88
Yarlside No.11 Pit, 95
Yew Crag, 59
Yew Crag Quarries, 57, 59

Zero Level, Force Crag, 121 - 122, 171, 173